# CAN GOD SAVE SAVE the Church?

*Living Faith . . .*
*. . . While Keeping Doubt*

# CAN GOD SAVE the Church?

*Living Faith...*
*...While Keeping Doubt*

— Kortright Davis —

WIPF & STOCK · Eugene, Oregon

Wipf and Stock Publishers
199 W 8th Ave, Suite 3
Eugene, OR 97401

Can God Save the Church?
Living Faith...While Keeping Doubt
By Davis, Kortright
Copyright © 1994 by Davis, Kortright All rights reserved.
Softcover ISBN-13: 978-1-7252-9520-9
Hardcover ISBN-13: 978-1-7252-9519-3
eBook ISBN-13: 978-1-7252-9521-6
Publication date 4/19/2021
Previously published by Hodale Press, 1994

This edition is a scanned facsimile of the original edition published in 1994.

*To the members and friends of
The Holy Comforter Episcopal Church
of Washington, D.C.,
on whose lively faith
and compassionate nurture
I have constantly relied*

# FOREWORD
## BY
## DR. MICHAEL A. BATTLE, SR.
### HAMPTON UNIVERSITY, HAMPTON, VIRGINIA

Can God Save the Church?

A striking question it is; but yet, a legitimate one that has little to do with the question of God's infinite power. While the verb "can" usually speaks to ability, this reference somehow has more to do with tolerance - tolerance from God that must be constantly directed towards those of us who make up the Church. God can indeed save the church; but will that church aggressively engage in that which constitutes salvation, or the result of salvation? But will the Church tolerate God's saving activity?

A striking question it is! It is a question that has long needed to be considered by both those who "practice" religion and those who preach religion. If we are to truly prepare ourselves to promote the practice of God in the knowledge of the complexion of God's thoughts and feelings, we must not only consider this question but also its profound implications on a theology that stands on the cutting edge of secular criticism. One must grapple with the reality, or lack thereof, of the effectiveness of that upon which the whole of society is based.

A striking question it is! It is a question that knows no denominational boundaries or creeds. While in this work the question is framed by the context of the Anglican Church and its episcopacy, it could well be raised by the historicity of all doctrinal practices whether they address a monotheistic or polytheistic reference to God and the resultant organism that embodies such reference. Can God Save the Church ... the Catholic Church; the Protestant Church; the Jewish Synagogue; the Moslem Mosque; the Hindu Temple ... Can God Save the Church?

A striking question it is! Not only must we consider the question; we must also identify and state the answer. If no other of the multitude of questions targeted at Christendom is ever answered, this one must be. To leave this question unanswered will strip the church of its mandate to make disciples, and to proclaim the Gospel as the power of God unto salvation. To do so would render powerless the apex of all power - social, political, educational and theological.

Dr. Kortright Davis raises with crystal clarity this question of tolerance; of faith; of commitment; of practice; of missions; of fairness; of theology. Notice, not of God; but rather, of theology - that body of information that we teach about God and with which we reference God. Davis challenges the reader to fulfill the God-given mandate for which the church was commissioned. He urges us, under the heading, Whose Mission Really Counts, to keep "... actively engaged in the unfinished task of witnessing to the Kingdom of God." He continues, "It is that which sustains the church in the value of hope in things not seen, rather than holding on to the many things which are seen but are not worth hoping for. If only we could see mission as the focal point of God's involvement in history, then the church would always be recognized as being the chief agency offering to the world faith, hope and love ..."

One cannot help but feel a sense of overwhelming relief as he reads through the chapters of this major work on the mission of the Church. Such chapters are: Can the Church Be Saved; God in Covenant and Change; (the above referenced chapter); Honesty Within - Prophets Without; Lest We Forget; Shape and Share the Vision; Christian Partnership for Social Change; Sweet Land of Liberty; The Church as Communion: in Faith, Life and Witness. Davis concludes this work with a most fitting admonition and appeal: "When we seek to isolate ourselves from the totality of God's loving created order, and withdraw from the frontiers of knowledge and creativity, it is then that we are overtaken by this sense of meaninglessness, and are quick to cry out in despair: "God! Save the Church!" But, when we take the risk of being fully involved with God's One, Holy, Catholic, and Apostolic mission, breaking new ground for the Gospel, and working with God in making all things new, through our radical repentance and constant obedience, the glories of God's brightness are most powerfully evident in the church's worship, work, and witness. It is then that the celestial angels rejoice with their unending song of praise: GOD SAVE THE CHURCH! May God's angels never cease to make their joyful song."

I unreservedly recommend this work for any serious worshipper who wishes to maximize his/her efforts in fulfilling the purpose for which the God of the church bought it into existence. If we fail in that mission, then the church fails. God, however, is saving the church now as He always has. The echo can still be heard: "... upon this rock I will build my church; and the gates of hell shall not prevail against it."

## TABLE OF CONTENTS

| | Title | Page |
|---|---|---|
| Preface | | xi |
| Introduction | | ix |
| Chapter One | Can The Church Be Saved? | 1 |
| Chapter Two | God In Covenant And Change | 15 |
| Chapter Three | Whose Mission Really Counts? | 33 |
| Chapter Four | Honesty Within - Prophets Without | 53 |
| Chapter Five | Lest We Forget | 71 |
| Chapter Six | Shape And Share The Vision | 77 |
| Chapter Seven | Christian Partnership For Social Change | 87 |
| Chapter Eight | Sweet Land Of Liberty | 103 |
| Chapter Nine | The Church As Communion:<br>In Faith, Life And Witness | 113 |
| Chapter Ten | God Save The Church | 131 |
| Postscript | | 147 |
| Endnotes | | 153 |

# INTRODUCTION

Can God save the Church? This might appear to many to be not only a bold and blasphemous question, but also a challenge to the omnipotence of God. It is not meant to be such, however. It should rather be taken as a quest, and not really a question. If the Church is traditionally regarded as one of the instruments by which God's saving will for the whole of creation is to be accomplished, and if the Church is to be that community which gathers into itself those who are being saved, do we not rightly expect that very Church to sustain within itself veritable signs that God's salvation is truly on the way?

If the answer is Yes, then a sense of the absence of such signs within the Church creates the urgency of the quest to find them. Further, such urgency also generates other questions about God's saving work in creation, apart from the Church, and about other signs of God's salvation coming towards those who earnestly work and wait for it.

Such are the concerns with which this book purports to deal under a number of different themes and by means of various encounters and opportunities for reflection. These concerns lie deep within the Christian heart which daily struggles for meaning, for new direction, for fresh words of assurance that the Christian way is still the right way after all. When the Christian community is rapidly distracted by socio-political and ideological issues, which often bear only a slight resemblance to what the original mission of the Gospel is to be about, then simple minds are forced to wonder if the prospects of salvation from sin and wickedness, and from evil and decay are to be placed on an indefinite hold. If salvation cannot be concretely assured within the household of faith - the Church, where else must God's faithful people turn to seek for such an assurance?

The material in this volume represents the ongoing struggles and reflections of one who has been attempting to discover various ways in which the meaning of Salvation might be practically explored. It evolves from a number of different situations and contexts over a period of time; and addresses itself to such themes as Salvation, Ecumenism, Higher Education, Social Change and Development, Early Afro-Evangelism, and Christian Social Witness.

For example, Chapter III appeared in an earlier version in *Crossroads Are For*

*Meeting*, (SPCK/USA, 1986). Chapters IV and X were delivered as the Stewart Lectures at the Seabury-Western Theological Seminary, Evanston, Illinois, in May 1993. Chapters V and VIII were sermons delivered in 1993, at St. Paul's College, Lawrenceville, Virginia, and Holy Comforter Episcopal Church, Washington, D.C., respectively. Chapter VI was first presented at a Provincial Consultation on Higher Education in Albany, New York, October, 1993. Chapter IX brings together material presented at two National Ecumenical conferences in 1992 and 1993. The themes may at first appear to be disparate, scattered, unrelated, and even irrelevant; yet they have one thing in common. Their common thread is simply the same enquiring mind and restless intellect of one theologian (myself), fully committed to the life of the Church, passionately involved in its ministry, and to its divine vocation to make a radical difference in today's world.

I must, therefore, bear full responsibility for any traces of foolishness, misguided thought, or factual error which these explorations may contain.

The material for this book has been brought together out of a wide variety of experiences and dialogical settings through which the underlying concerns of the author have continued to surface, and through which they have been explored with a spirit of radical enquiry and incisive investigation. They pose far more questions than they ought, and they suggest fewer answers than they might. Nevertheless, the nature of the quest is not to be found so much in finding the right answers, nor the right amount, but rather in shaping the questions in the right way in the hope of stimulating some forms of wider dialogue and genuine Christian concern.

For if indeed the Christian life is still to be understood more in terms of a pilgrimage than of an arrival, then it is in the nature of such a pilgrimage that we seek to raise the right questions at the right time and in the right way in the sure and certain hope that God will help us on to the next stage by providing faintly provisional answers, just for now. Further, the title of this volume seeks to portray the mind of one who would engage in a process of wrestling - theologically, ideologically, historically, and relationally - within the context of a community of faith to which one is unswervingly committed, and with a God who not only takes pleasure in springing surprises, but also seems to delight in attracting such wrestling anyhow.

This is the lingering clue about the divine reality which one picks up from a Jacob who refuses to release the messenger of God; or from a Gideon who plays many tricks to make sure about the God's will; or from an Elijah who wins a contest but still runs away like a loser; or even from a Nazarene carpenter who cries out on a cross after having summoned Lazarus from his four-day sleep of death. Wrestling with God, and with questions about God, means that at the very least, we are prepared to take God seriously.

Thus, questions about the shape and nature of the Church, about the efficacy of God's saving work, both within and beyond the Church, are questions which lie at the very roots of Christian faith. The lively Christian does not lose faith by raising them, or by refusing the easy simplistic traditional answers. The Christian of lively faith, in

*Introduction* xi

taking hold of a reasonable and soundly inquiring disposition, puts faith to work in the midst of living doubts, thereby making for existential enrichment and purposeful commitment to the possibility of a more glorious future. "Living Faith While Keeping Doubt" makes doubt itself more constructive of faith, and renders Christian witness far more exciting than the tangible and bankable rewards would seem to suggest. All of this comes together, one hopes, in the basic question: **CAN GOD SAVE THE CHURCH?**

At a time when the witness and work of the Church seems to be coming under constant attack from sources within its own ranks, when the ideals of the Gospel of Jesus Christ are being systematically questioned by those who would offer easier solutions to the complex problems of human life, the Church is being called to think again. When the paradoxes of modern living are steadily complicated by the ironies of religious contradictions, and when the ethical norms and standards of the Gospel are overwhelmed by some compelling forces of pragmatic materialism and hedonistic spirituality, new frontiers must be charted for the work of the Gospel and people of faith.

Can the Gospel break new ground? Is it really true that the faith which goes out to work is the faith that really works? Can the preaching of the Church be heard with a new freshness? Where are the new religious leaders being trained? What do they learn, and what is expected of them when they assume leadership in our churches? What has become of the so-called decades of Development in which the poor have grown poorer, and the scandals of materialism have continued unabated? Where are the new frontiers for the Church as the 21st century dawns upon us? Are there new alliances to be formed between religion and health, or must the linkages between religion and politics continue to hold sway?

These and other questions call for some concentrated reflection and discourse; we need to engage in some discussion on them, and on related issues. What are the ethical, practical, missiological, and theological imperatives for a faith that is wholly committed to following Jesus Christ as Lord and Savior? This volume is, therefore, an attempt to make some contribution to the debate about the witness of the Church at the dawn of the 21st century, and to explore some new ways of looking at the mandate of the Gospel with which the Lord of the Church has entrusted it. I can only hope that those who take the trouble to read it will encounter some sources of godly irritation that will indeed trigger their own modes of enquiry and struggle as well as strengthen their own lines of quests and questions.

Kortright Davis
Howard University School of Divinity
Washington, D.C.
June, 1994.

# CHAPTER ONE

## *CAN THE CHURCH BE SAVED?*

Can the church be saved for the next century? This is undoubtedly an awkward question for today's Christian; for it assumes that the church is either in bondage, or that it is likely to be. Yet, today's awkward questions will be the obvious questions tomorrow; but the freedom of the church, in its various contexts, is still not an obvious fact today. We need to begin some explorations into this question by looking at the contemporary context and its implications for the immediate future.

### *OBSOLESCENCE GUARANTEED*

We are often made uncomfortable when we are reminded of the fact that nothing lasts forever. The principle of life which constitutes our universe remains very constant in its operation. Life is like a complex drama of gases. The astronomers remind us of the way gases behave - they emerge, they expand, and they expire. William Shakespeare's imagery of the world is that of a stage with its exits and entrances; with all men and women merely players; with many parts to be played by each actor until he/she has no further part to play. We need to be reminded, therefore, that whether or not we build obsolescence into our systems - physical or metaphysical - such obsolescence is guaranteed. But can obsolescence be delayed? Can the disintegration of our finest efforts be postponed?

The answer must clearly be in the affirmative given the massive scales of creative achievement which we have witnessed in the twentieth century. The tremendous surge of the creative human spirit has accounted for the human mastery over countless threats to human life and livelihood - hunger, disease, ignorance, drudgery, and inefficiency. If ever there was a time when the human claim of having been created in the image of the Creator-God could be persuasively substantiated, then the present century merits that pride of place. Yet, as we stand on the commanding heights of human creativity and view the landscape of our proud accomplishments, we are still haunted by the spectacle of the darker sides of human behavior.

This has been the century of two devastating World Wars. This has been the century of massive genocide, unprecedented militarism, and mindless terrorism and violence. The baser human instincts which fan the flames of greed, sex, injustice, and the abuse of power have all been refined into sophisticated structures of social acceptance and tolerance. It is almost universally conceded now that the unbridled pursuit of such instincts is no stranger to any sector of social leadership, not even European royalty. The shades of darkness resulting from human creativity, or the misuse of human freedom, are further increased by the realization of a constant spirit of Mutually Assured Destruction (MAD), under which our inhabited planet exists. We now have the power to wipe out all human life within a very short space of time; such is the level of our nuclear efficiency.

Those who preside over this power assure themselves that it is merely a deterrent, and seek to assure others (at least by inclination) that they really have no intention of using it. Nevertheless the power exists, and the threat of a nuclear holocaust exists - with its devastating effects on the minds of our younger generations. It is imaginable that the holocaust could be initiated by default rather than by design; there could be a misreading of signals or a malfunctioning of systems. We live in the throes of the supreme paradox that those efforts which we have made to secure ourselves from being destroyed by others can in fact trigger the means of our own self-destruction. Our point of super-strength lies at the threshold of our deepest vulnerability, and we move relentlessly towards the next century with this odd sense of security.

Security has many forms and offers many roads towards its realization. The preoccupation with national security which sovereign states display is perhaps indicative of the common concerns for personal security which absorb so much of the time, energy and resources of modern living. The question may well be asked whether the diverse concerns for security, which are expressed in systems of every description, are in fact the modern way of working out the meaning of human salvation. Theologically speaking, is there any direct correlation between the security systems of the modern world - personal, social, industrial, national - and the basic human need for salvation? Are we attempting to save ourselves, or at least attempting to secure the means of our preservation? We should make a very clear distinction between the basic human need for self-preservation, and the basic human quest for such means. It is the constant dialectic between this human need and the human quest, in the context of the guaranteed obsolescence of human systems, which seems to constitute a significant part of the religious agenda for the future. Questions about God, the Church, its mission and prophetic role in the world are basically contingent on the broad implications of this dialectic.

The rising tide of the illicit drug industry and culture, the proliferation of cults and groupings all in search of meaning and self-fulfillment, the collapse of the moral authority of some ecclesial systems and pronouncements and the questionable support of nationalistic insurgent activities by foreign governments, all combine to render this last decade of the twentieth century a period of great disillusionment and uncertainty for some people.

In such a pervasive climate filled with terror, fear, trepidation, human pain and suffering, physical destruction, military conflagration, and ecological degradation, not only are people unsure about what to believe, they are also unsure about whom they should trust. Loss of trust and respect always creates fresh forms of bondage and despair. So that when the structures of trust and credibility begin to crumble under their own weight, then the institutions in service of human welfare, and the social instruments engaged in ensuring human survival are threatened with obsolescence. Salvation is postponed.

Modern humanity continues to struggle for meaning and salvation. In the face of apparently overwhelming powerlessness and pointlessness, humanity holds tenaciously to the belief that salvation, although postponed, is still possible through a Source which transcends human arrogance, and prevails over systemic obsolescence. This Source is symbolized by the idea of God which, although it is often in bondage itself, refuses to disintegrate. We, therefore, need to turn to the question of God as an area of theological exploration for the future of emancipatory value and meaning in the human family.

## "GOD": FROM ANSWER TO QUESTION

Perhaps one of the most significant points of recognition to emerge out of recent missiological studies and research is that God has never been, or can never become, a part of the message and cultural baggage which missionaries claimed to have taken with them from the North to the South, or from the West to the East. Earlier claims of taking the God of light to dispel the devils of darkness in other cultures have now been partially abandoned. Those who, in missionary settings, claimed that God was the answer have now begun to recognize that God has always been the question - the question that addresses itself to every cultural context, whether or not that context has been confronted by other cultural modes.

A former American missionary to China, J. Herbert Kane, recounts his experiences in that great country with these words:

> "The Communists made a big mistake. They got rid of the missionaries but did nothing about God. He stayed on when the missionaries left; and when we were out of the way God went to work, in his own way, by his own power, for his own glory; and the end result is beautiful beyond

*anything we could have imagined. From many points of view, the Churches in China are the strongest and purest in the world today.*"[1]

It is not merely in the field of missionary endeavor, however, that the transition of the idea of God from answer to question has taken place. Social structures which were once undergirded by a presumed understanding of the divine will have been cracking, and lines of distinction based on class, race, sex, wealth, nationality, intelligence and the like, have lost their halo in the wake of radically new outpourings of human concern. The hitherto fixed orders of rights and privilege have been called into serious question; so that even poverty, hunger and darkness of skin, are no longer treated as symbols of divine disfavor or displacement. To hear rich white people claim to have seen Jesus in the faces of poor black starving children of Haiti or Somalia is to provoke the question about what they were seeing before.

Most significantly however, the transition from answer to question has also taken place in the world of the theologians. Theology itself has witnessed a new form of emancipation. Ecclesiastical leaders have either been challenged, or have challenged themselves to re-state what they really believe about God and Jesus Christ. Ordinary men and women, struggling to put their faith to work in an alien and oppressive context, have reached new realms of religious understanding and spiritual awakening where their own religious teachers have not. The words of the psalmist have found fresh meaning: *"I have more understanding than all my teachers, for your decrees are my meditation."* (Psalm 119:99, NRSV) There is in popular theology today a new death-of-god articulation which authentically reflects the workings of a force over which no human agency or institution can claim any control. It is the death of "God" as the answer from the North; for the many traditional answers to the problems of human oppression have not really delivered on their promises. God the question remains; it challenges every form of response to reality as it is perceived. Reality wrongly perceived leads inexorably to unreality strongly believed.

As we move towards the start of the twenty-first century then, not only are people questioning what they have always claimed to believe, but they are also acting out that questioning in new forms of social behavior and personal relationships. There are radical departures from received forms and customs, and systems of value are being transformed in the multiple search for new meanings in life. There is no guarantee that the new meanings will be better than the old, but it is clear to them that the basic question about ultimacy and self-fulfillment (the question about God) still needs to be satisfied. It is precisely on the point of ultimacy in life, and emancipation for full humanity, that the question of God persists. In the light of this question, therefore, we need to explore the trends which currently suggest themselves.

## PRESENT QUESTION - FUTURE TRENDS

It has to be more than a coincidence that in the century when we have witnessed the rise of materialism through two radically competitive ideological forces - atheistic communism and deistic techno-capitalism - Christianity has increased statistically from being the fifth largest to being the largest world religion. The expansion of Christianity has in part been due to the dominance of Western capitalism, in part to the fight against an eventual collapse of communism, and in part to the witness of faithful Christians across the globe. Effective Christian witness through mission and evangelism has indeed created a deeper and yet broader sense of what it means to be the church. Nevertheless, the "evils" of communism and its variations, coupled with the material success of capitalism and its alliances, have brought about an inordinate assimilation between Christendom and the Gospel in the modern mind. The obvious irony is this: that which should constantly be under the judgement of the Gospel has often succeeded in keeping the Gospel itself in captivity. The present question, therefore, is whether the Gospel can be set free from Christendom without damage to the church and the Christian faith. The future trend is that without such an emancipation of the Gospel the future of God's mission for the church might be increasingly difficult to discern. In the light of this proposition, certain trends may well be already on the way. Let us briefly identify some of these trends without engaging in any lengthy discussion on them.

The nature of religious experiences has been so universally understood to be non-denominational (except perhaps the claims about visions of the Mother of Jesus made almost exclusively by Roman Catholics) that the acknowledged source of such experiences must also be de-denominationalized. The church as a whole will need to become more active in its proclamation that "God is no respecter of persons." That is to say, the God of the Christians is not a Christian. The understanding of the nature of God, let alone the talk about God, will become less Western, less dogmatic, and de-institutionalized.

Throughout the communities of the Christian church around the world, there has emerged a wider plurality of theologies, each claiming divine guidance and enlightenment. Enough verbiage has already been expended as to indicate that the church is at war with itself - theological warfare is being waged on many fronts. Clashes of cultures and ideologies have been over-laid by conflicting claims of exclusive rights to the discernment of divine truth. Out of all this will emerge a pluralism of approach and witness to the Apostolic Faith, and a new generation of believers who will no longer be threatened by the decentralization of authority, or by the pluriformity of styles and structures in the church.

The largest body of Christians has also indicated some trends of major significance. Roman Catholicism has managed over the centuries to maintain itself on the strength of some structures - papacy, celibacy, dogma, tradition, uniformity, monasticism, mission, and sacramentalism. These have provided a centrifugal force in spiritual, moral or political matters. However, Catholicism itself is being radically transformed from within. The reformation in North America, the revolution in Latin America, the abdication in Europe, the thrust for liberation in Asia and the indigenization in Africa have all provided overwhelming evidence that Roman Catholicism is under reconstruction. No one can confidently predict its future shape or force. The coming new shape of Catholicism (for even the label 'Roman' is being abandoned by some Catholics) will have a significant effect on the rest of the Christian church.

The twenty-first century is sure to witness the emergence of a new attempt to reconstruct the modern personality as a result of the bankruptcy of modernism. The attractiveness of aggressive individualism in almost every sphere of human endeavor will lose its appeal because of the high casualty rate in human relationships. Thus the reconstruction of modern personality will begin with a struggle for the rediscovery of human virtues and modes of relationships. It will place primary emphasis on the supremacy of communitarian principles, and bring greater restraint to the baser instincts of the human species. The reconstruction of the modern personality will also give rise to three very significant movements for change.

First, there will be a greater concerted effort to mount the struggle for the liberation of human life from the tyranny of technological power. Second, the current patterns of ethnocracy around the world will be drastically realigned. For example, the industrial prominence of the Japanese today will continue to generate bitter conflicts between themselves and the Americans, especially as the latter have been unable to retool themselves for industrial efficiency or social discipline. Or, again, with the inevitable transformation of the South African society, new alliances between African states will create ripple effects in the geo-politics of the Third World, and the geo-economics of the Industrialized West. Third, even if the current classification of the so-called "Worlds" is likely to remain in place, (First World and Third World), the management and exploitation of resources, coupled with the modification of forms of international protocol and suasion, will inevitably set the under-classes of the world free from the stigma of inherent inferiority. In other words, Third World peoples will one day become first class citizens of the world. If God does not do it in the next century, then the humble and meek may yet succeed in exalting themselves.

Besides all these considerations, it is confidently expected that major challenges brought on by shifts in demography, technology and ecology will create some radical dislocations of value and virtue in the next century. No one can safely assume that the balance of power, or the distribution of successful effort, will maintain the present configurations.

What then about the churches in the next century as far as their organizational behavior and political emphases are concerned? If the foregoing prognostications merit validity, then there are some inescapable consequences for the churches as they seek to function in their societies, and to mirror in large measure whatever is considered to be of worth and significance. For example, the social structures that are currently sanctioned by the churches will surely collapse and make way for new candidates. Class determinations and social priorities will be modified in the light of the reconstruction of the modern personality; and things that mattered so much before will be quietly forgotten or extinguished. This refers particularly to matters of sex and sexuality. The inevitable de-mystification of sex in the decades to come will create new forms of mutuality and allegiance, and the politics of sexuality which dominate the psyche in the corridors of the highest ecclesiastical leadership will undergo a process of radical transformation. In this regard, it is likely that reform in sexual politics will precede theological consensus or ecclesial approval; for in matters of this nature the absence of genuine theological response often renders the political initiative inevitable. Theological politics are always much sharper and more precipitous than any brand of political theology.

It is through a focus on social reconstruction that the issue of the church's mission plays out its strongest possibilities. For if we contend that social reconstruction is not only desirable, but also possible and inevitable, and if we believe that God takes the world seriously - for the God who creates the world is also the God who saves the world - then God's mission for the world, through the agency of the church, is essentially salvific and emancipatory. We have already looked briefly at the question of human security and salvation, especially in the context of the guaranteed obsolescence which characterizes our existence. We have noted that in the face of such characterization there still persists the question of God, as that which relates to the human quest for some alignment with ultimate reality, and for self-fulfillment. The future trends do not in themselves suggest that salvation will be any nearer or clearer in the future than it is at present. Should the mission of the church be abandoned then, since there seems to be nothing to show for all the toil and sweat of missionary witness and evangelistic endeavor? The answer must lie in the negative since God has disclosed no deadlines for the eventual success of what is ultimately a divine enterprise. God's time is continuous, without count and without measure, and we need to interpret the church's missiological agenda on the eschatological grid of divine intention and the glorious consummation.

## The Mission Of Salvation

We have grown accustomed in theological circles to dealing with the ancient claim of Cyprian: *"Extra ecclesiam nulla salus."* ("There is no salvation outside the Church.") The question in the title of this chapter is in direct confrontation with that dictum when it asks the question - "Can the Church be saved?" It used to be the premise that salvation was only available through membership in the Christian church, and that God had no other salvific strategies available of which we were aware. The missionary enterprise was, therefore, urgent and necessary since no Christian should be complacent about the prospects of eternal damnation for those who had not been evangelized and baptized. Now that we have begun to allow that God may (or must) indeed have other means of salvation, the question of salvation and the church has taken to the spin. Ecumenical dialogue, and other forms of collaboration between persons of different faiths, have made it impossible for Christians to treat non-Christians as candidates for Hell. Is there salvation outside the church? The growth of a stronger affirmative answer to this question is one of the brighter marks of religious and theological relationships at the present time. But where will such affirmation lead?

The future of God's mission can only be affirmed in the light of what has been previously understood by Christians to have been revealed through the Scriptures. The Biblical foundations of God's mission can never be in doubt since the God of the Bible is the God who continues to meet us in the incarnate and risen Christ, and also in the church which is God's sacramental community. That sacramental community is also a missionary community sent by God to continue the work of Christ. What is that work of Christ? It is the work of the Spirit - who is God in the nearness of creation. Thus we can say with the South African theologian, the late David Bosch, that mission is "the church's participation in the work of the Spirit to renew the face of the earth".[2]

It is this participation of the church in the work of God's Spirit which places a distinctive meaning on the nature of mission itself, and of its scope for the future. We will focus much more attention on the mission of the church in Chapter Three.

It is nevertheless important for me to make the point here that the doctrine of God is as missiological as it is soteriological. Who cries to a God who cannot save, who cannot emancipate us? Who takes seriously a God who cannot deliver what is needed? Questions about the future, security, ultimacy, self-fulfillment and social reconstruction are always before us. The need for a God who saves is strongly indicated, particularly throughout the church itself which was once seen as a bastion against the countervailing forces of evil and despair in the world at large.

Can the church then be saved? It all depends on the soteriological axis along which it seeks to move. Can the church as a pilgrim community, gathered together by bonds of common faith in Christ, be emancipated from the insecurities of modern living? Can it be liberated from the effects of the guaranteed obsolescence with which modern life has to deal? Can it be set free from the inevitable trends which human relationships at varying levels have already put in train? Can it be released from any obligation to participate in the work of social reconstruction? Can it be saved from itself? The answer to all these questions is no. No, the church cannot be saved either from itself or by itself; for it is heavily enmeshed in a complex web of crises.

The Franciscan theologian, Walbert Buhlmann, has offered a catalogue of problems which he says some consider to be symptomatic of a "great deal of harm in the (Roman Catholic) church." These are: "a mass exodus of priests and religious confusion in theological teaching, insubordination among the laity, an erasure of the boundaries between Catholicism and Protestantism or even non-Christian religions, and finally, an absorption into the secularized world."[3] While it is difficult to understand why the erasure of boundaries between Catholics and Protestants should be a sign of harm in the church, especially as the founder of Christianity (the Nazarene Carpenter) was neither Protestant nor Catholic, it is still interesting to observe how strongly the feeling of crisis is being felt in the minds of those who speak out of the denominational context of the largest sector of the Christian Church. To make matters worse, however, Buhlmann claims that Roman Catholic authorities are out of step with current realities. "Rome," he says, "is desperately swimming against the tide."[4]

Yet, as goes the Roman Church, so too does much of the wider family of Christians in their organized and institutional life. The crises which they face can be witnessed in some degree or other in most of the major churches throughout the West. Where there is less evidence of these, however, is in the predominantly Black churches in the Western hemisphere, and in the basic ecclesial communities throughout Latin America. In these two significant groupings there can always be found a vast majority of those for whom the church is the main measure of their life, their sense of belonging, their cause for hope and liberation, even their means of interpreting the realities of their socio-historical condition. For most of these people, the word "church" is a verb rather than a noun. To do church is to seek life in much of its fullness, and it is this inextricable association of church with life which gives them a fresh understanding of what it means to be led by the Spirit, and thus to be on fire for Christ. It is very clear to any careful observer that the whole church needs to listen to what the Spirit is saying through such people, regardless of their color or social status, and not to regard them as fringe-like exceptions to the traditional norms. The church cannot be saved without them.

As an instrument of God's salvation, the church participates in that which is both mysterious and yet real. As it seeks to make known God's love for the world, and as it seeks to remain open to the fullness of the Gospel of forgiveness and emancipation, it is radically confronted with the broader dimensions of what the mystery of cosmic salvation entails.

The Indian scholar, P. Devanandan, has reminded us that "Christ's judgement and salvation is social and cosmic and includes also the world of science and technology, politics, society and culture, secular ideologies and religions."[5] The World Council of Churches Bangkok Assembly of 1973 proclaimed that salvation involved four major points of focus: Economic Justice, Human Dignity, Solidarity against oppression, and Hope against despair. No human mind can fully comprehend the true meaning of salvation - either in terms of what we are to be saved from, or the means by which we are to be saved. Neither can we presume to determine when salvation-point has been reached. At most, we dare only to speak of salvation as a divine-human process, and on that basis we have certain indications, through God's revelation in Jesus, about where that process must necessarily lead in concrete and historical terms. The mission of the church is to work out in very concrete ways what is the nature of God's emancipation which it seeks to offer to others. That mission is to share in the reconstruction of social realities through the rediscovery of God's mission to itself first. It is the rediscovery of God's one, wholly catholic, and apostolic mission.

Such a theme is being consistently expressed by theologians in different contexts across the globe. For example, one South African scholar says:

> "It seems to me that our priority now is not to 'reach the unreached,' but to 're-reach the reached,' to re-evangelise the Church (and therefore ourselves). Our most urgent calling in an oppressive and violent situation which could become a full-scale civil war is to my mind not to Christianise 'pagans' but to humanise Christians and thus to make our contribution to the attainment of that justice which will make peace possible among us."[6]

We might also add that we Christians ourselves need to be 'de-paganized' in so far as we engage in a praxis of oppression and injustice in total contrast to the call of the crucified Christ and all that he stands for in the divine economy of emancipation.

The very important work of the church will continue to be that of strengthening its faithful witness to the Gospel, particularly within its own fold, by striving against endemic forms of evil and disobedience to the divine will. Racism, injustice, greed and old-fashioned God-almightiness will continue; but the church that attempts to make any compromises with such manifestations of the anti-Christ cannot be an instrument of, or a participant in, God's assured work of salvation. So that, in the final analysis, the direct answer to our question, 'Can the Church be saved?' is simply 'Not on its own terms.' The tragedy of the present century is that the church has allowed itself to lapse into a false sense of assurance that it can both offer salvation, and can itself be emancipated on terms which it can negotiate. God's salvation is God's alone, and no other source can dare claim prior rights or privilege.

## ECCLESIAL SALVATION AND THE PROPHETIC ROLE

Is there then a prophetic role for the church? The tradition of prophecy has always been related to individuals rather than institutions as such. The prophet is one who is seized with a certain consciousness of God's demands and God's justice, and thus proclaims by word and witness the inherent imperatives of such a divinely inspired experience. The prophet warns God's people and God's nation, and tells forth the likely implications of any situation which persists outside of God's righteous and covenantal demands. But what happens when God's authority is seen to be compromised within the church itself? What happens when the dominant cultures among Christians virtually reduce the idea of God to a privatistic notion of self-perception, or cultural preference, or individual conscience? Who really cares when the church presumes to warn the nation in the name of God? Social developments in post-Christian Europe have called into serious question the traditional claims of European and Euro-American Christians to superiority in human value, or possession of moral and religious rectitude. It is said that the rumor of God is fading in the countries of the North, while the presence and power of God still radiate in the countries of the South.

Let us return to Buhlmann's reflections for a moment. He asks the question:

> "Furthermore, even in Europe and North America, once the time is ripe, why may we not experience an invasion of the same Holy Spirit who has turned so much to the good over the last twenty years in Latin America, Africa, and Asia? If I speak of the Holy Spirit, of course, that does not mean that we should sit on our hands waiting for a little 'coup d'etat of the Holy Spirit'."[7]

How does Buhlmann consider that something new can be done? He contends that "modernity seems badly lacking a moral rudder," and that perhaps the church might pursue the "new" Ten Commandments from God, which he outlines as follows:

1. You Will Allow Common Sense to Prevail.
2. You Will Take Yourselves Seriously as People of God.
3. You Will Extend Your Hand to Your Fellow Christians.
4. You Will Take Sides with the Poor.
5. You Will Wonder at the Breadth of the Creator.
6. You Will Acknowledge That the "I Am Here" Is Present Among All Peoples.
7. You Will Accompany Religious Nomads.
8. You Will Swell the Ranks of the Peacemakers.
9. You Will Make the Earth a Paradise.
10. You Will Encounter the God of History.[8]

While it is true that these "commandments" are primarily addressed to the Roman Catholic Communion, there are clearly many insights which they proffer to a much wider Christian audience.

Can the church then be saved? If so, what is its prophetic role? In addition to Buhlmann's "commandments," let us consider a few areas of prophetic witness for the church if it would attempt to take God's salvific and emancipatory designs seriously.

First, the church will need to demonstrate prophetically that healing is possible in a broken world, chiefly by becoming more and more a healing and compassionate community. By offering to the world a new way of accepting God's reconciling grace, which is in effect to embrace the brokenness of God in Jesus, the fracturedness in post-modern society can be challenged.

Second, the church will need to take seriously the on-going threats to human livelihood - the restlessness of the young, poverty, injustice, human rights violations, atheism, child and spousal abuse, oppression of women, and family collapse. These threats need to be addressed systemically; for they erode the very foundations of human dignity.

Third, the church will need to develop ways of relating pastorally and prophetically to the political directorates of our time without fear of repression, or overweening arrogance. Chaplaincies may be effective for organizational harmony, but other modes of more effective witness and service are urgently indicated.

Fourth, the growth in religious pluralism will itself create a new prophetic task for the church. The fact that God is not a Christian is itself grounds on which the church might seek to offer prophetic witness for the reconstruction of modern society. Collaboration with persons of other faiths, or with persons of no faith, is not merely an optional extra for Christians, it is of divine necessity.

Fifth, the nature of the church as a pilgrim community ('paroikos') makes it imperative that the provisional nature of codes, canons, and styles of conduct be emphasized. God's salvation is as continuous and progressive as it is cosmic. It engenders mutual participation and genuine fellowship. No understanding of the divine-human relationship can therefore afford to be fixed or exclusive. Provisionality is enjoined at every stage because of God's ongoing self-disclosure.

Sixth, the church will need to persist in its call for the participation of the people in the management and control of their own affairs as an inescapable demand of genuine human freedom. No society can be considered just where laws are made and codes are enshrined on the behalf of people whose participation in the process is totally excluded. Belief in God's creatorship demands acceptance of, and respect for, human pro-creatorship, and no sector of humanity should command a higher status than any other in God's economy.

Finally, the modern forms of theological initiative are almost all seeking ways of understanding the meaning of emancipation from all forms of bondage, and of working out in practice what such emancipation requires. Pragmatism has historically been a philosophical and ideological system of the zig-zag, fraught with ambiguities and difficulties for the ethicist. The prophetic role of the church will demand the charting of new forms of Christian praxis, provided always that Christian praxis does not give comfort to the unethical demands of any socio-political system of modern pragmatism.

As the church continues on its pilgrim path through history, trying to discover in the midst of many crises what it means to be the body of Christ, the people of God, the sign of the Kingdom of God, the trends for the future are clearly being indicated by the social and historical realities of our time. The church must be conscious of the fact that although salvation is assured by God, it cannot save itself; nor can it serve the world without some serious attempt to provide a prophetic witness as a counter-culture, and become engaged in emancipatory praxis on God's behalf. Such a self-understanding is not possible without a genuine renewal of that inalienable sense of the contemporary context in which the confessing church, as the witnessing people of God, seeks to interpret its mission as being authentically divine.

We, therefore, need to turn immediately to an exploration of the theological significance of the nature and character of God as it has been understood in the history of Israel in particular, and in world history in general. The God of Israel has been made known through a covenantal relationship with God's elect; but Israel's God has also been made known in world history through radical social change and human transformation. The God who is known is covenant and change is the God who constantly beckons us to repentance and renewal in all dimensions of our life. What all this means for us in terms of Christian witness and service will hopefully assume greater significance as we move on to such a discussion in our next chapter.

## CHAPTER TWO

## *GOD IN COVENANT AND CHANGE*

No one likes to be cheated in the market-place, and yet hardly anyone passes up an opportunity to accrue some gain or profit, sometimes even at the risk of a little cheating here and there. The business of deals and contracts, of exchange and services, of getting and spending, is all part of normal human intercourse and transaction, and it is made all the more acceptable and attractive when we stand to gain far in excess of the presumed value of our outlay. In short, we all love a bargain, it adds spice to life.

Life in the political sphere is quite consistent with our attitudes in the field of commerce. Political activity generally involves the need for exploring new levels of compromise and accommodation whereby parties of differing persuasions might jointly score gains from the opportunities of the political moment. There are those who would contend that politics is an art - "the art of the possible." Others prefer to regard it as a science - "the science of deals." Whether we confine politics to the realm of art, or of science, we are nevertheless constrained by the fact that it radically affects every aspect of our relationship with each other. It also determines much of what we plan for ourselves and our charges in the cause of social access and the promotion of human livelihood.

Political contracts are taken for granted within the framework of legal conventions and constitutional arrangements. They are implied in the civic rights and privileges which we espouse and defend. They are fundamental to our understanding of personhood and property. They undergird the spirit in which we try to conduct our social affairs with dignity and decency; and yet, to be overtly political is to merit the disfavor of our fellows. They still prefer to suggest that politics is a necessary evil. To be human is to be a political animal; it is to be enmeshed in the network of contracts and deals, without which the body politic would be ungovernable.

What then of the life of religion? If there are bargains to be grasped in commerce, and contracts to be managed in politics, by what arrangements do we conduct our religious affairs? While it is possible to translate the symbols of commerce and politics into concrete factors ... for example, a simple piece of paper (a check) procures a large vehicle (a truck), or a single vote in a machine helps to determine who signs bills into law ... the religious process depends upon the quality of a reverse procedure. That is to say, we conduct our religion by converting concrete factors into symbols - whether of language, ritual, or imagery - and those symbols are thus expected to signify a level of reality which can in no other way be articulated or validated.

The symbols have no objective validity. They carry only such meaning as we choose to designate for them. They provide for us the pointers to ultimacy and absolute value which not even the life of politics or commerce can approximate. Does this mean then that we carry within ourselves a sort of duality of existence which enables us to respond to two different sets of needs and value? Or does it mean that we combine within ourselves some gradations of existence so that while we may function politically we still remain religiously submissive to invisible higher powers whose favor we regard as indispensable for our salvation? It is the role of culture to function as the integrative force which draws on all aspects of our existence, whether sacred or secular. Culture determines the value of our symbols while it gives texture to the shape of our language. Language is made in our own image.

There is perhaps no other word that so integrates the power of culture, commerce, religion and politics as the word "covenant" - "foedus" (Latin), 'berit' (Hebrew), 'diatheke' (Greek). It is, therefore, not surprising to recognize that in the traditions of the ancient world the language and life of covenant permeates most of the social fabric of human relationships and expectations. Our main concern will be with the language of covenant in the Israelite religion as we seek to identify the theological antecedents for the use of the concept of covenant in Christian theological reflection.

A covenant is basically an agreement or solemn promise between two persons or groups of persons; it is bound by an oath either through some verbal formula or symbolic action. Covenants as international and social treaties were extremely commonplace in the ancient world; they were the lifeblood of relationships in ancient political and social life. A close perusal of ancient covenants tells us a great deal about the life, times and character of the contracting parties. We learn much about the historical contexts in which they functioned, their norms of behavior and their social customs, their rituals and their religious ideas and ideals. We need to remember that they were by no means unique to the life and religion of Israel.

Indeed, the work of G.E. Mendenhall, Delbery Hillers and Gary Herion, among others, has placed the language and structure of Israel's covenants firmly within the scope of other ancient treaties. Mendenhall and Herion insist that even among the Hittites of the Late Bronze Age, the covenant, or the treaty, "was merely a device for communicating values envisioning human relationships proceeding along some moral plane higher than coercive force."[1] It is difficult to determine whether other ancient peoples, besides the Hebrews, entered into a covenant between themselves and a deity. The significant difference seems to consist in the notion of kingship. Only Israel acknowledged their God as their king, at least in the earlier phases of their history. Our main concern then is about the nature of the relationships between God and humankind, and about the power of the language employed in understanding that relationship. Yet, we must not be unmindful of the fact the Israel's covenant with God had some unique features which distinguished it from other international treaties.

## COVENANT THEOLOGY AND THE OLD TESTAMENT

Covenants abound in the Old Testament. God makes a covenant with Noah, Abraham, Phinehas, and the Davidic dynasty. There is the central covenant with Moses at Sinai (Horeb), the covenant of Joshua, the covenant of King Josiah, as well as the covenant of Ezra. They all span the historical spectrum of Israel's growth and development from being a tribal league in the desert to becoming a nation, and eventually a cultic community. The constitutional arrangement of the desert eventually becomes the formulary to be recited in the Jewish liturgy. At the base of it all there was the covenant which so radically depicted Israel's relationship with God in a most objective and dispassionate form. It was the covenant that brought law and history together, and eventually placed law over history. The covenant placed Israel's God far beyond any notion of divine caprice, and made the relationship between God and Israel understandable in human form. Israel's God had revealed a loving initiative in calling her into a unique community with relationships, obligations, and exclusive loyalties, which marked out a distinctive divine character in history.

There can be little doubt that covenant ideas continued to emerge as Israel's society evolved, and that the multiplicity of covenants in Hebrew sacred literature is attributable to the constant updating of the understanding of the nature of Israel's God in the social and political life of the nation as well as in its religion, of course. Did Israel ever take these covenants seriously? It is not easy to determine this. To understand religion and religious obligation in human form is to rely on the language of metaphor, and this metaphor of human relationship, the covenant - whether through commerce, law, culture or religion - enabled Jews, and later Christians, to transcend several contradictions inherent in the story of human experience.

Let us look a little closer at the varieties of Old Testament covenants. First, the covenant with Noah in Genesis 9, expressed the human faith in Yahweh as the God of nature, the God of creation. God's sovereignty over the natural order was a direct corollary of the belief in God as Creator. In that covenant God was thus being self-bound by certain patterns of a creator's choices that would redound to the lasting benefits of God's creatures. Second, the Abrahamic covenant in Genesis 15 (J tradition), or Genesis 17:1-14 (P tradition), denoted human belief in Yahweh as the God of history. God would be limited by certain historical efforts through Abraham and his offspring; through them would Yahweh become 'God of the Earth' and all the inheritors of Abraham's faith would be blessed. Third, the covenant with David in II Samuel 7, established the royal dynasty while the covenant with Phinehas in Numbers 25, established a legitimate priestly line. Less is traditionally made of the latter than of the former. What is important to observe about the Davidic covenant is that David's blessings had actually preceded the covenant itself - the blessings were thus to be realized by his descendants. It was in a very real sense a product of the pre-Messianic era, and it represented "a vision of hope likely to survive the disappointments with so many historical descendants of David."[2] It must be noted, however, that the three covenants just mentioned have sometimes been referred to as "charters," since in each case no agreements were made between parties, but rather a catalogue of rights and privileges is granted to the individual by God in solemn charter. God binds "Godself" to these men in divine charter.

It is chiefly in the light of the Sinai Covenant that the covenant of Joshua (Joshua 24), the Josianic covenant (II Kings 23), and the covenant of Ezra (Nehemiah 9), are to be seen and understood. Indeed, no other covenant is as formative to the life and religion of Israel as the covenant with Moses at Sinai. Wellhausen's view that the covenant was simply the logical concept which the prophets used for conveying religious truth and affirming ethical obligations has in more recent times been superseded by a more cogent understanding of the role of covenants as formative instruments of communities in the Late Bronze Age. The covenant gave form and structure to the social and religious life of the early community, until it eventually became more of a symbol, since law tended to characterize the political structure of the once covenant community. The relationship between Yahweh and early Israel was like that between a suzerain and his vassal. But Mendenhall points us to a radically new understanding of the meaning of this covenant in the context of Israel's contemporaries. He says this:

*"The transference of suzerainty from a flesh-and-blood emperor to a supreme and unique deity was not only a religious revolution; it was simultaneously a protest against the feudalistic imperialisms of that time, a religious expression of the human striving for freedom from an oppressive external political control and exploitation. It was also a development of the utmost importance for the history of religion, for it placed moral obligations above political and economic interests in the scale of religious values."*

While we would be misguided in thinking that the covenant concept lost most of its fundamental importance as Israel attempted to grapple with the challenges of becoming a theocratic nation-state, we would also be remiss in ignoring the attempts during certain phases of later Jewish history to re-establish the core of a religious community based on a return to the old covenant of Sinai. For example, the community of Essenes regarded themselves as the faithful inheritors of the new covenant relationship between Israel and God. Their <u>Manual of Discipline</u> contained many legal stipulations reminiscent of the old Israel, although they regarded themselves as "the community of the eternal covenant."[4] The Essenes were thus a sincere community in Judaism; "yet for all their sincerity, Essene ideas about covenant are essentially conservative and recapitulate familiar patterns. Their new covenant is a renewal of the old."[5]

Recent Jewish scholarship has done much to place renewed emphasis on the main theological implications of the Sinai covenant for the life of Judaism. The work of David Hartman in his book <u>A Living Covenant</u> has been most instructive. His basic argument is that "a convenantal vision of life, with mitzvah (divine commandment) as the central organizing principle in the relationship between Jews and God, liberates both the intellect and the moral will."[6] With respect to the Sinai Covenant, Hartman points us to three dimensions of theological significance that are explicit in the relationship between God and Israel. First, there is the freedom and spontaneity of God. Second, there is the reality of human freedom, coupled with the acknowledgement of divine self-limitation. Third, there is God's interaction with humans in history, and God's choice to involve them in determining the course of their history. These theological dimensions are not only significant for contemporary Judaism, they are also of fundamental importance to the Christian understanding of the divine-human relationship. Hartman emphasizes the importance of mutual commitment and the integrity of the other, thus ensuring separate existence as well as separate rights. He points out that the covenant does not denote a mystical union with God, but it rather characterizes a fusion of relational self-understanding and autonomy. This stress on autonomy is very important for Hartman, for therein lies the basis not merely for human freedom but also for human responsibility.

What then about the issue of redemption? Does the covenant make any such ultimate guarantee? Hartman is quite explicit at this point. He says -

> *"The covenant of Sinai points to the ever-renewed possibility of beginning the spiritual process. It does not give one certainty regarding the ultimate direction of history. Mitzvot are significant not because they point to or make possible a future redemption, but for the quality of life they make possible in the present. Human finitude and the sense of being a creature separate from God remain permanent features of the religious life. Faith does not give one an anchor point through which one transcends the finite human situation."*

Christian theology differs from Jewish theology at this point, chiefly because of the assurance which faith in Christ, as a gift from God, provides for the believer. The final outcome of history is already assured, the cruciality of the crucified and risen Christ provides the foundation on which it is possible to transcend the finitude of any human situation. The Christian hope enables the believer to interpret the relationship with God in terms of final redemption.

Perhaps it is this low level of faith and absence of radical hope implied in the Sinai Covenant that causes the prophet Jeremiah and the writer of Malachi to look beyond its constraints to something more. We have already spoken of the Qumran Community, the Essenes, who saw themselves as the members of the new covenant community. The concept of the new covenant was derived chiefly from Jeremiah 31:31-34, where the prophet predicts that it will be a new covenant of the heart, radically different from the Sinai covenant. It would be a covenant of forgiveness of sins as well as a deeper sense of the knowledge of God. Scholars have repeatedly pointed out that this concept of the new covenant in Jeremiah was never taken up again in the literature of the Old Testament. The other looking forward is to the "messenger of the covenant," in Malachi 3:1. The covenant referred to here is that between God and Phinehas (or Levi), the covenant of the perpetual priesthood. And yet the hand of an interpolator seems to be at work, if we are able to follow the scholarship of Bruce V. Malchow. Malchow argues that this passage shows that the Israelites of his day (the interpolators) awaited the future coming of a priestly messiah, especially because of the disruptions of the high priesthood under Antiochus Epiphanes and after. He notes that in the Pseudepigrapha, e.g. <u>Testament of Twelve Patriarchs</u>, the image of the priestly messiah becomes a full blown figure.[7]

## COVENANT THEOLOGY AND THE NEW TESTAMENT

It has been suggested by Mendenhall that for a little while the early Christians regarded themselves "as a community bound together by covenant, but that this covenant [was] a most free, creative reinterpretation of the older traditions."[8] There were of course serious religious and political difficulties to be faced. For example, Christianity was in no way an extension of Judaism and the Mosaic laws. Furthermore, secret societies were illegal in the Roman Empire, and a covenant was regarded as such. Mendenhall therefore suggests that eventually "both the astounding creativity of the early Church and the radical break with Jewish forms and associated patterns of thought very soon produced a structure of religious thought and life in which the old covenant patterns were not really useful as a means of communication, and may have been dangerous in view of the Roman prohibition of secret societies."[9]

If the centrifugal story of the Old Testament is the miraculous escape of the Jews from Egypt, then the centrifugal story of the New Testament is the death of Jesus of Nazareth at the hands of the Roman authorities, and the affirmation of belief in his resurrection. Both are, in their own way, stories of salvation which speak directly about the nature of God and of God's activity. The story of the Exodus is followed by the establishment of the Sinai covenant, the creation of a new people of God. The death of Jesus, as God's activity, is also followed by the creation of a new people of God -

a spiritual community, empowered and enlivened by the Spirit of God, and by faith in Christ who, being raised up from the dead, is regarded as "the mediator of the new covenant" (Hebrews 9:15). The celebration of that death is symbolized by the sharing of the cup of the new covenant through the blood of Christ - the Eucharist is continuously the 'anamnesis,' the re-living of the death of Christ until he comes again. Mendenhall and Herion draw our attention to the close connection in the early Church between covenant and sacrament in the Eucharist, particularly in such factors as the binding together in oath *se sacramento obstringere* (Pliny) through the use of bread and wine, and through the 'anamnesis,' the calling to mind of the death of Jesus. They suggest that "the Eucharist by and large could have been little else but the participants' *sacramentum* ('oath') in which they actually submitted to the lordship of Christ (i.e., to a transcendent, extra-social authority; the 'kingdom of God').[10]

What then is the shape of covenant theology in the New Testament? Do the Christians adopt the old covenant traditions under a new dispensation? Do they fulfill the requirements of the Mosaic Law by yielding to a higher level of legal obligation in the law of the Spirit? Do they constitute the new Exodus community out of which the new covenant becomes the formative factor in their relationship among themselves, and between God and themselves? Klaus Baltzer argues thus: "In their formal structures the old and the new covenants do not differ. The new element in the new covenant is its historical foundation."[11] This seems to me to be reading far more into the 'covenant' metaphor than is required for the understanding of the Christian relationship with God, chiefly because there exists no formal community of Christians out of which a formal covenantal structure could emerge. The action of baptism into the Christian community was the symbol of re-birth, while the circumcision of the Jewish male was the concrete affirmation of a birth that was already experienced. To equate baptism into Christ with circumcision into Judaism seems to me to miss the essential nature of one's baptism into the death and resurrection of Jesus; for it is the re-birth into the spiritual community for which no formal structure can exist. Do Christians then share in a new covenant? Hillers has this to say: "The Essenes had a covenant, but it was not new; the Christians had something new, but it was not a covenant."[12]

But it may well be argued that Paul makes use of the language of covenant in Galatians and II Corinthians, to the extent that he speaks of himself and his colleagues as "ministers of a new covenant" (II Cor. 3:6). What we need to pay attention to in this regard is that the concern of Paul at this juncture is not with the "new covenant" as such, but rather with "the new life of the spirit." At the point where Paul recognizes the sharp contrast between the two religious dispensations - the old dispensation of condemnation, and the new dispensation of righteousness - the new dispensation is that of the Spirit. The Spirit is the Spirit of Christ; it is a new bond, a new covenant, but it is a bond of freedom. *"Now the Lord is the Spirit..."* writes Paul, *"... and where the Spirit of the Lord is, there is freedom."* (II Cor. 3:17). Paul thus combines Christ, Spirit, freedom and covenant, not in a new covenant relationship but in a new experience of the presence of God who sets free all those who are in Christ. "Covenant" thus spells new life of assurance of freedom in the context of the life of the Spirit. In short, we have in the New testament not a new covenant at all, but a radically new understanding of the covenant metaphor, which can in some way establish new patterns of understanding for the meaning of the new life in Christ. Mendenhall and Herion suggest that the covenant in New Testament thought points to the new ethic of the rule of God, "freed from cultural parochialism and political arrogation that inevitably accompanies a defined code of norms and laws."[13] The mystery of God's saving action in Christ beckons the use of many metaphors. What is at stake is to determine their value and significance. It is the metaphor of "covenant" in the New Testament which points to "the radical transformation that constituted the early Christian Church," and which "remains an excellent example of what can happen when new wine is put into old bottles."[14]

## COVENANT AS METAPHOR

Our discussion on the Biblical use of covenant has helped to articulate an understanding of the nature of God, who is the God of Abraham, who is the God of Moses, who is also the God of Jesus. We have spoken of the sovereign Lord of creation, who is unconditionally free and righteous, transcending all limitations of creatureliness, perfect in holiness and mercy, intimately involved in history, making promises and keeping them, absolutely trustworthy and faithful, demanding proper standards of human justice and obedience; and, in the face of it all, utterly self-limiting and creatively riskful with what is created. This is a God who is responsible for the final outcome of the whole created order, and yet who is understood to be partial to those who by election and promise are in a special relationship with God. This is a God who strikes a bargain with individuals, groupings and dynasties, and who makes possible the means of renewing arrangements that have fallen through. This is a God who never gives up, who keeps on trying new ways of reconciliation, until in the end the spectacle of a sinless and innocent carpenter/prophet being nailed to a cross by Roman functionaries signals the supreme religious claim by a half-Jew, half-Roman citizen: "... *God was in Christ, reconciling the world to himself...*" (II Cor. 5:19). Was that the spectacle of a new bargain, a new way of establishing a deal between God and humans? Was it a final demonstration of the bankruptcy of all deals between God and humans? Or was it rather the supreme historical symbol of the real relationship between Creator and creation? I firmly believe that it was.

From the standpoint of contemporary Judaistic thought, Hartman contends that the "convenantal mode of the spiritual life challenges the individual to live with the tension between the dignity of the autonomous self and the unswerving commitment to the community."[15] The importance of the community and the obligations inherent in one's membership of it cannot be over-emphasized in Judaism. Yet there is that strong individualism which has to be nurtured not only by membership in the community, but also for the strengthening of that very community. Covenant in this way is at one and the same time an exclusive/inclusive spirituality that undergirds the self-perceptions of the private/public person. But the metaphor lacks universality and global wholeness at this level. It cries out for an eschatological dimension of life which alone can confront the otherwise time-bound tendencies of human domination and ultimacy. The metaphor requires an encounter with spheres of human freedom which transcend the boundaries of any existing community.

Charles S. McCoy, in his book When Gods Change: Hope For Theology, speaks of the covenant concept as involving a network of commitments, and a wholeness of human experiences. He says that ordinarily, covenants of human living have to do with creation, consummation, coherency, and spheres of reality - "they give shape to human communities and action."[16] McCoy emphasizes that the nature of community has to take seriously the realities of pluralism and the constant need for liberation. By attempting a theological reconstruction which uses the federal (or convenantal) paradigm, he says that theology can set itself free from the traditional confines of the Western Constantinian paradigm, and respond more authentically to the just demands of theologians from differing cultural and contextual orbits. McCoy extols the virtues of the convenantal (federal) paradigm with these words:

> *"Covenant faith emphasizes communal memory and loyalty within which we grow to selfhood, and at the same time draws us toward a future of anticipated liberation. Covenant means liberation, and liberation provides the criterion to measure movement and to discern a pattern of faithfulness when the gods change."*[17]

While Hartman speaks of covenant as a mode of spirituality, McCoy speaks of it as a paradigm for theological reflection. Both emphasize its utilitarian value for the promotion of community, and for the anticipation of a better life within the community. Neither seems to indicate that the concept of community itself stands in need of transformation. The pluralism of McCoy and the individualism of Hartman both ignore the fundamental factor of personhood. Because Christianity is essentially an incarnational religion, and because the crucial factor in human living is the possibility of becoming full persons in accordance with what is meant by the "image of God," we need to take into account some understanding of the divine-human relationship which relates to the possibilities and pain of personhood. Although we dare not suggest that anthropology is of the essence of religion in general, or of theology in particular, we are nevertheless constrained by human concerns to reach out into the realm of those things which concern us ultimately as human beings.

In the midst of the grammar of ultimate concern then, we are naturally confined to the use of symbols, signs and metaphors, which must bear the weight of the concerns we have. Our concern with being persons, and with becoming full persons, carries with it the notion of transcendence, as well as the belief in an encounter with another personal presence more powerful than our own. It is this overwhelming sense of the presence of God that is sustained by a faith in the risen Jesus, through the faithful and historical witness of the Christian church. Christians do not believe in the idea of the resurrection; they believe in God who raised Jesus from the dead, and whose permanent presence is actualized in history. None of this would be possible without some measure of a transcendental human personhood. J. Philip Wogaman is therefore right when he suggests: "Is it not because the transcendental character of human personhood, taken as the basic metaphor for ultimate reality is continuously open to new experience and moral sensitivity, while at the same time remaining fundamentally rational? The divine-human relationship can be seen as a continually unfolding one, just as human relationships unfold ... Convenantal faith relates to the center of being as personal, not as conceptual ..."[18]

No other aspect of human personhood so manifests the transcendental character of the person as the possibility of freedom. No other aspect of the Christian faith so completely enshrines the meaning of freedom as the genre of the divine-human relationship as the resurrection of Jesus. The resurrection is thus not merely God's act in Jesus, it is supremely God's bargain and ours in the unfolding drama of divine freedom and human responsibility.[19] Covenant itself is set free from law and regulation, and the Cross is the question for which the empty tomb provides the ultimate answer. God's commitment to human freedom is irrevocable.

## GOD'S BARGAIN AND OURS

The biblical witness strongly attests that the covenanting God, the God in relationship with humans, is also the God who is continuously involved in self-disclosures. Slowly, mysteriously, yet surely, more of the character of that God is disclosed. Quite often, such disclosures are made possible when human beings - as persons of faith - are at critical phases of their lives. Slavery in the New World caused the slaves and their descendants to receive divine self-disclosures which slave-holders never shared. The horrors of war in the twentieth century have unwittingly produced new avenues of spiritual enlightenment that are otherwise inexplicable. Persons of faith are constantly bombarded with a combination of human concerns which may be represented by the following words: Presence, Promise, Providence, Pain, Power and Permanence - the six 'P's. Together they constitute the extent of the bargain for which human beings in their finite existence are always searching. Can they find it in a relationship with the God of Abraham, Moses, and Jesus?

Human life is always beset by a complex of complexes. There is, for example, the complex of evil in all its subtle, brutal, technological, bureaucratic and ideological manifestations. There is the complex web of dependency which robs the human spirit of the power of self-reliance and security. There is the complex network of creaturely relationships which breeds flights of fantasy and despair as well as phases of loving trust and warmth of affection. There is the complex of weakness and fear which controls so much of the human apprehension about the present and the future. Above all, there is the complex of death with all its proleptical enslavement and powerlessness, and with all the constant reminders and warnings of its certainty. How can we, in our limited humanness, survive all these complexes, unless we seek to strike a bargain of freedom, a bargain of transcendence? It is the nature of the Christian Gospel to demonstrate that faith in the God of Jesus is in itself a divine gift of freedom, bound up with the Christ who belongs to God. Such is the freedom that creates anew and saves; it does not destroy. The New Testament faith is that it emancipates the believer from the slavery of sin, the slavery of fear, the slavery of the threat of death, the slavery of the law of self-interests, and the slavery from the power of the complexes to which we referred earlier. We are thus emboldened to work out with some measure of assurance, within the covenant community of faith in Jesus Christ, how this gift of freedom from God translates itself into a bargain, both for God and ourselves. We can explore this bargain of freedom in the light of the six over-riding concerns; the six 'P's mentioned in our previous paragraph.

As a bargain of the Presence of God, the believer is assured of a forgiveness of sin; for sin hitherto brought about spiritual estrangement and a sense of alienation. The bond of divine-human relationship is a bond of a transforming and reconciling presence, which sets the believer free to worship and to witness as a new participant in the resurrection appearance. The Christian can authentically testify - "We have seen the Lord." No second-hand testimony can be authentic.

As a bargain of the Promise of God, the Christian believer has the historical witness of Israel and the Apostolic Church. God always fulfills God's promises. More often than not the measures of fulfillment come in unexpected ways, but nevertheless they do come. What is important here in the promise of God as a bargain is that the believer, as a free moral agent, can safely choose to trust in the trustworthiness of God. Such trust demands human responsibility and moral rectitude, not as a condition of God's fulfillment, but as a demonstration of the meaning of the divine-human relationship based on trust. Knowledge of a trustworthy God inherently requires responsive obedience and faithful witness to that trustworthiness.

As a bargain of the Providence of God, the Cross of Jesus Christ constitutes the most powerful historical symbol of God's involvement in human affairs. For while the Cross represents the worst potential of human power, it also demonstrates the strange contradiction in divine providence. Death becomes not the end of life or the final meaning to life; it becomes, rather, the triumph over human injustice and weakness. Most of the problems experienced in our lives usually raise the question of whether they are deserved or not. The Cross denotes for us that questions of just desert are ultimately divine considerations, and that the chances of our natural destruction do not impede the overall purposes of God's saving will for us. The bargain of divine providence enables the frail human spirit to rise above the awful spectacle of death and destruction.

As a bargain with human <u>Pain</u>, God assures the Christian believer that God in Christ also suffers. It is the nature of the divine-human relationship that God is not unmoved by the suffering and discomforts of the creaturely partners. It may well be asked: How is it possible for the supreme and sovereign creator to suffer? What has become of the traditional doctrines of divine impassibility? Does this not reduce theism to a crude and palliative anthropomorphism? On the contrary, the move is in the opposite direction, for it helps us to understand pain and suffering in theomorphic terms. It is impossible to maintain a belief in a transforming and reconciling divine presence which is untouched by the realities of human finitude. The nature of the divine self-limitation requires also a belief in a God who suffers - not only <u>for</u> us, but <u>with</u> us. The Christian grammar of love, as the central character of God's nature, is quite unambiguous about the meaning of a creative and redemptive love which shares in our suffering in some way or other.

As a bargain with <u>Power</u>, God in Christ discloses to the believer the power of love as the absolute creative power. To accord ultimate status to transient arrangements is by far the most demonic of forces within human relationships. The powerlessness of the human spirit is never more severe than in the belief in the unlimited power of another human spirit. The rise and fall of civilizations and cultures never seems to satisfy and re-assure us that all human power is relative and transient. The power of God at work in the spirit of ordinary men and women, and in the light of the resurrection of Jesus, and in the witness of the spiritual community - the church - signifies the bargain that we have with God that the gates of Hell shall not prevail.

As a bargain of <u>Permanence</u>, God discloses the nature of the relationship between God and humanity. It is unconditional and absolute on God's side. It spells eternal commitment and final consummation. On the human side there is the quality of hope and surrender, of constancy and renewal, of commitment and privilege, all of which give to life its meaning, its value, and its responsibility. The meaning of freedom takes on a dimension of divine significance, for we are understood to be free to become those whom God wills us to be. It is in the life of the church, as the community of the resurrection, that the bargain of permanence is enacted through word and sacrament, and through the practice of witness and service in concrete situations. It is in the life of the church that the fulfillment of humanity in its wholeness is to be expressed, and where the full arrival of the new creation is to be eagerly anticipated. Although the church remains the pilgrim people of God, there is still an assurance of divine-human permanence which transcends experiences of change and renewal. This assurance of permanence does not in any way suggest that God is not powerfully revealed in the changes of history. We will shortly be turning our attention to this aspect of the covenant God.

Where then is the community that should provide the context for such a network of bargains? The community is formed out of the commonality of concerns and expectations, but it is not delineated by any human structures, or constitutional, or cultural arrangements. Paul is right when he attributes to the Spirit of God the formative factor in the divine-human relationship - as many as are led by the Spirit of God are God's children. So that if there is covenant, it is the covenant in the Spirit, and if there are bargains, they are bargains of the Spirit. We are joined together by the Spirit, and in the Spirit, and there is no way of validating the boundaries of such a covenant community. God then is not bound by *our* spirit; rather *we* are bound by the Spirit of God - and to be so bound is to share in the vision of the "shalom," the steadfast will and purpose of God through which the world of faith responds in solidary love and hope-in-action.

For just as God has no guarantee against our misuse of human freedom - the failures, uncertainties, and unpredictabilities will always be experienced - so, too, do we have no guarantees against the consequences of human finitude. All this is of the nature of the bargain. At the very least, we have the assurance that God's nature will not change on us, God remains constant and free to be God. Hartman reminds us that "while the covenant does not promise that the ambiguities of history resulting from human freedom will be eliminated or that we will overcome the limitations of our finitude, it does give us the courage to begin again, so that failure need never weaken our resolve to strive to reinstate the sanctifying power of the covenantal norm."[20]

The language of covenant is no longer anthropomorphic, but theomorphic; for God has radically transformed the meaning of human terms through the resurrection of Jesus from the dead. It is fundamental to our self-understanding as an emancipated convenantal community. To quote from Mendenhall and Herion again:

> *"Covenant is not an 'idea' to be embraced in the mind, and therefore religious community cannot be defined with respect to 'orthodox' appraisals of that idea. Covenant is an 'enacted reality' that is either manifested in the concrete choices individuals make or not. The rule of God is defined with respect to those whose concrete choices arise out of certain positive values that actually transcend culturally bound norms and politically enforced laws."*[21]

We are therefore inheritors of a freedom which is both a bargain with, and a gift from, God. We remain fully assured that in the dispensation of the new creation there is no power or presence that can ever again separate us from that love of God which we together experience through the Spirit in Jesus Christ our Lord. Yet the covenant God, who is the source of our freedom, is also unconditionally free - free to be involved in a covenant of love and salvation, free to be known as constant and unchanging, and yet free to be authentically disclosed in the changes of human history. The God of Jesus is known both in covenant and change. It is to the paradox of this divine self-disclosure in the midst of change that we now turn our attention.

## Changing God - Unchanging World

As we attempt to explore the theological implications of our belief in a covenant God who is known in the changes of our historical experiences some fundamental theses and biblical themes form the basis for our discussion.

Six basic theses will be suggested here without any discussion. They are as follows:

a. God is known by what God has done.
b. God is also a God of surprises.
c. The history of God's salvation is no different from the history of God's creation.
d. The meaning of Christ for today evolves out of, but is not identical with, the meaning of Christ yesterday.
e. Sin and salvation are both dynamic in time, and cosmic in scope.
f. The Christian church, as a community of the Spirit, is both mystical and mysterious, and its members cannot always predict or recognize the surprising moments of the Spirit.

Then there are six biblical motifs which speak to us of a changing God.

First, <u>The Flood</u> (Genesis 6: 1 - 8):

In spite of the greatness of the human species, the giants, and other outstanding appearances of greatness, there were other factors. Human corruption prevailed, the human order was rotten. God contemplated the change (Verse 6), and repented of the original creative act. Noah alone seemed acceptable. The lesson here was that human <u>corruption</u> should not be tolerated, it must be washed away, eliminated in the Deluge.

Second, <u>The Exodus</u> (Exodus 15: 1 - 18):

The Exodus is not to be seen in isolation from two other important historical factors. On the one hand there is the experience of slavery and oppression in Egypt which makes necessary God's deliverance of the oppressed. On the other hand there is the sequel of the Covenant relationship and responsibility which binds the newly liberated people in a sacred community. The lesson here is that one cannot claim the Exodus experience without having known one's Egypt, or without accepting the demands of the Covenant. <u>Slavery</u> manifests itself in many modern forms - some subtle and sophisticated. Yet God stretches out God's saving hand to change such conditions by Emancipation and Exodus.

Third, <u>The Exile</u> (II Kings 25: 4 - 12):

This was a very striking turn of history that the same people of the Covenant had become devastated, and the magnificent symbol of the presence of the Covenant God (the Temple at Jerusalem) was destroyed. Was it divine retribution or human unfaithfulness? Israel regarded it as the result of <u>alienation</u>. The God who was known in changes allowed even the sacred Temple to be destroyed. The lesson here is that alienation breeds exile. Yet Israel's strong sense of the faithful God of the Covenant does not admit to any sense of "Ichabod" (the glory has departed). God's glory never departs from God's faithful.

Fourth, <u>The Return</u> (Nehemiah 2: 9 - 20):

The zealous faith of Nehemiah may be interpreted along ethnic lines, along religious lines, or along nationalistic lines. He was a butler (cup-bearer) in the household of Artaxerxes. There was more to him than the king could recognize in his countenance. Nehemiah suffered the pain of <u>obscurity</u>. The changing God empowered the faithful remnant out of such obscurity and gave them a renewed sense of identity. The lesson here is that God always names God's own by calling God's people into being. Christian identity is always experienced in our being called by God out of darkness into light. It is a daily transformation in which we continue to meet God afresh in the changes of our existence.

Five, <u>Apocalyptic</u> (Daniel 11: 1 - 4):

The function of apocalyptic in literature is always very significant as a response to actual history. It is both liberative and evocative. It emerges out of the agony of oppression and dependence. Something must change. God must work the change sometime, sooner or later. Whenever history becomes dehumanizing, there is some element of faith required to identify even the smallest sign that change is on the way. God's faithful live out God's apocalypse in history, living <u>as if</u> freedom were already there. The lesson here is that we are to become who we are, in spite of the countervailing realities in our present experience.

Six, <u>Easter</u> (Matthew 27: 45 - 53):

Nothing could be more dramatic a statement of fact than that the changing God is not bound by time, place, space, or energy. There is only one hour on God's clock, and that is the Now. Thus the supreme miracle of <u>transformation</u>, the resurrection of Jesus from the dead, takes place in the very heart of the crucifixion. God eternally changes the meaning of the death of Jesus, and also that of our own. It is clearly not resuscitation. It is not a conjuring trick. What happens, we do not know. The fact that we are committed members of the church seeking to further the work of the Gospel is perhaps sufficient proof in itself that the resurrection of Jesus is real. God is known supremely in the transhistorical fact of Easter. Easter people worship a God who meets them in the changing of Death into New Life.

Through these six motifs, at least, the biblical witness thus points us to the fact that we worship a changing God, and that such worship embraces the totality of our lives. However, we most powerfully experience the ongoing activity of God as both emancipatory and sustaining when we are confronted by such factors as corruption, oppression, unfaithfulness, social obscurity, events beyond our control, and even our own mortality. God is always changing, and as we are determined to struggle for liberation from such conditions, so God's enabling and transforming work is made plain in many ways. It is made plain in the midst of the change from bad to good, death to life, old to new.

The changing God is also affirmed in a number of other existential changes. These changes are continuous; for they constitute a dialectic without which the realities of life and the promises of the future would be impossible for us to articulate.

For example, there is the dialectic of between Chaos and Creation. God's creativity takes place principally in the context of chaos. Wherever chaos is indicated, the Christian knows that God's creative activity is already on the way. When things are neatly packaged and systematized, the experience of the changing God is postponed, for God is not pre-packaged nor culturally pre-conditioned.

There is the dialectic of Change and Conversion. Whenever the sense of change for the better is being experienced, whenever there is a move out of the realm of evil, there also comes into being the need for conversion, a turning to God. Conversion is not just a punctilear operation in time, a once-in-a-lifetime experience, it is a daily act of the believer. Every stage of conversion points to the need for more change, and thus for more conversion.

There is the dialectic between Growth and Disorder. The experience of the early church is historical proof of this. As the church grew, so much the more it gave the appearance of disorder and confusion. The trials and errors of the first four or five centuries of its history attest to this. There seems to be no divine-oriented growth without a strong sense of human-originated disorder. This is not necessarily a bad thing, since we are reminded through Paul's spirituality that God's strength is made perfect in our weakness. In any case, people with the tidiest kitchens are not generally the best cooks; nor are professors with the neatest offices usually the most productive.

The significance of the church as the people of God is always held in constant dialectic with the in-breaking of the Kingdom of God, of which the church is called to be a principal sign. Thus the people of God are always being called out of themselves so that they might faithfully respond to the coming Kingdom of God, and so demonstrate what such a Kingdom should look like in historical terms. Yet the church is not the Kingdom of God, and the need for the church to keep on changing towards becoming more of a sign of its coming involves radical changes and constant adjustments. Thus, "People of God" and "Kingdom of God" are always in a fertile and constant dialectic.

Further, the entire biblical and theological enterprise takes place within a concrete historical context. It is world-based, but it also claims to be world-saving. There is so much that helps us to recognize that, in spite of all its imperfections, this is the world which God loves, and in which God chose to become incarnate. We are therefore believers in a world-affirming God, even as we seek to make ourselves more prosperous and comfortable in a God-disaffirming world. This is not merely a dialectic between sacred and secular, between good and evil, or even between church and world. It is a dialectic within our very selves, out of which we struggle to make sense of a world that offers fewer signs of God's creative love while we continue to proclaim the vital need for that very love.

Thus, in a world that appears to be changing, we come to the stark recognition that it really is not. It holds relentlessly to what it considers to be the basic constructs of its nature, such as, Chaos, Corruption, Individualism, Oppression, and Evil. Yet, the God who seems to be the immutable One is actually the changing One. God is experienced chiefly in the changing scenes, the paradoxes, and the dialectics of life. It is, therefore, as we face up to the implications of what God calls us to become, and what God does in the context of our sense of the need for change-for-the-better, that we can reaffirm our faith in the Christ who was designated as such through that most radical of all changes, his resurrection from the dead. The resurrection of Jesus is the basis of the New Covenant into which God calls us forth to mission and salvation. For the modern Christian, the most powerful proof that God really exists is not found in the arguments or in the biblical texts; but rather, in the faithful living out of God's changing us from the old way to the new ways of the Spirit. None of these can adequately be defined; they can only be vigorously enjoyed. Christians are those who catch the Spirit, and who move forward with complete confidence into God's glorious and ever-changing future.

In conclusion, there is always the need to revisit our roots, to take fresh soundings of our religious foundations, to re-examine our sense of vocation, and to seek fresh mandates for our Christian work and witness. We know that the God who is known in the changing is also the God who is known in the calling. The covenant God and the changing God are one and the same. The God who calls us forth also sends us forth in mission. But mission strategies which try to be evolutionary without being revolutionary remain faithful to the Gospel of Pragmatism, but not necessarily to the Gospel of Jesus Christ. Radical change is painful, costly and disruptive; but no new life really emerges without it.

# CHAPTER THREE

## *Whose Mission Really Counts?*

The world is full of missions and missions. There are missions into outer space; there are missions to the center of the earth; there are missions into jungle territories; there are missions into places of turmoil; there are missions into areas of the unknown. There are missions authorized and missions unauthorized. There are secret missions and public missions. There are foiled missions and missions aborted. We live with missions all around us. But do we also live in mission? Whose mission really counts after all? Is this not the question which radically affects the nature of the church and its offer of God's salvation to the world?

Theologically speaking, can there be mission without the church? Or can the church function authentically without mission? Which is unthinkable without which? Are they integral to each other; or is it the endless Christian task to work towards the full integration of both? What are the implications involved in regarding them as separate? And what are the consequences of treating them as identical? These are our present concerns. Let us first reflect on what mission means.

### *The Meaning Of Mission*

Our understanding of the word itself suggests that "mission" has something to do with "sending." It always involves movement, and it is chiefly an activity between persons. Normally we think of mission as having four aspects - first, the sender; second, the person sent; third, that which is to be done by the person sent; fourth, the resulting effects of what has been done. It is possible to speak of a "personal mission" in the sense that an individual sets for him\herself a special task or goal; but perhaps in such cases the concept of mission is incomplete. One could seriously argue that a so-called self-imposed mission was only a manner of speaking about one's own ambitions and aspirations, or even a symptom of a dual personality. Be that as it may, we simply wish to posit at this time that mission involves a sender and a person sent with something to do.

This multiple aspect of mission dominates the true meaning of the prophetic tradition in the Old Testament, and also gives to ancient Hebrew religion a very unique feature far beyond the reach of its contemporaries. The great figure of Moses which throws its bright beams of light back to a Babylonian old man points us to these words: *"So Abram went, as the Lord had told him; and Lot went with him. Abram was seventy-five years old when he departed from Haran (Genesis 12:4)."* Those bright beams also enable us to find two cousins at the river of Jordan arguing about who should be baptized by whom, and then the eventual words from a third party from above: *"This is my beloved Son, with whom I well pleased (Matthew 3:17)."*

So, the God of the Old Testament is One who sends, and the covenant relationship, which is understood to be in effect between God and God's chosen people, seems to carry with it, for all time, the component for mission. This missionary component does not appear to be locked into the institutionally arranged order of things. It comes to the fore in strange and unexpected ways, so much so that there are times when the officers of the covenant ritual, the priests, seem unable to determine whether a mission is authentic or not. The prophets always seemed to be standing outside of the institutional framework while, at the same time, they called for a return to the original relationship which the covenant produced. No wonder then that Jesus of Nazareth is recognized as an outsider by his own people, and is eventually disposed of as such. Nevertheless, his claim was that his mission was not to destroy any of the religious tradition, but to simply fulfill it. We must notice that he is never credited with the notion that fulfillment meant either institutional reform or expansion, but only a radical shift in relationships and perspective. The Great Commission of Matthew 28, is given on the top of a mountain, and is reminiscent of the law-giving activity of Moses. The question of authority for mission is not in doubt, it belongs to the same Covenant-God who is also the Lord of Creation. The teaching, preaching, disciple-making and baptizing must be done in the name of that God whose presence is always assured.

We must notice how the first generations of Christians chose to carry out their missionary task in faithful response to the Lord's commission. First, they went about proclaiming the Easter story, and calling on their hearers to repent and be converted. Second, they developed small and manageable communities of believers - they encouraged the growth of household churches. Third, they used the current means of communications, and produced kerygmatic literature for aiding their missionary task. It is out of this that we have our lasting treasure in the New Testament. Fourth, they were not afraid to give their lives for what they were proclaiming with their lips. Christian martyrdom was a most effective missionary tool. We need only recall the connection implied in the Acts of the Apostles between the stoning of Stephen and the conversion of Saul of Tarsus. All of this was the missionary strategy of the early church.

The meaning of mission continues to be a debate of enormous proportions in Christian circles today. What is the Christian attitude towards non-Christians? What does mission mean in relation to peace and justice? What is the missionary task towards other Christians? What is relationship between mission and growth? All of these are questions which concern every Christian, and indeed, the non-Catholic world has in these last decades been actively engaged in dialogue and action to discover, and to demonstrate, what is the authentic meaning of the Great Commission of Jesus in the light of contemporary realities.

How should we proceed to understand what mission truly is? There is a real and urgent need for us to find some way of conceiving and proclaiming the most appropriate response to the Gospel today. An earnest attempt to address it will surely help our cause in the dynamic integration of mission and church. For the Gospel is about forgiveness and freedom; it is about life in all its fullness; it is about faith and food for the whole person in the whole world. The Gospel says that God is Bread, and Jesus speaks of himself as the Bread of life. The foundations of the Gospel are characterized by a religion of mercy and compassion, and Christians today speak out with boldness about the grace of God that has been experienced in the world in general, and in the church in particular. There is a very real sense in which we are to acknowledge by faith that world history and salvation history are identical; for the God who is still creating the world is also the God who alone is saving it.

Ion Bria rightly suggests that mission must be understood as an actualization of "God's economy in the midst of the world, by a community which is by its nature a 'sign' of that economy."[1] What does this mean for mission as we are to understand it? It means surely that mission is central to Christian theology since it springs out of our understanding of the very character of God, rather than out of either the doctrine of the world, or that of the church. The mission is always God's mission and, at best, the church merely participates in it. The church neither defines nor reforms it; it is essentially God's activity. True mission can neither originate with the church, nor can it point only to the church.

A number of considerations flow from this. First, the basis of mission is that self-disclosure of the solidary love of God in creation, redemption, and fulfillment. Second, the trinitarian disclosure of God as Creator, Emancipator, and Sustainer, means that God's mission is cosmic in scope. Third, William Frazier is on the right track when he suggests that the purpose of mission is to discover the purpose of mission.[2] Fourth, we begin to see what mission is not. For example, mission is defined by origin rather than by objective. It is neither church extension nor religious proselytism, but it is God's actualization in history; for in Christ it is demonstrated that God takes the world very seriously. It is not primarily concerned with conversion and individual salvation, but with the redemption of the whole world. True mission arises out of an acknowledgement of our unconditional and responsive dependency upon God, rather than out of any radical allegiance to a particular institution called church. True mission then is a sign - a sign of witness that God's kingdom is already on the way, already being established as a present reality in the world of personal experience and human relationships.

The witness of the church is a living sign of the kingdom, and that witness is expressed in proclamation, fellowship and service. But mission is much more than that. It is truly an exegesis of history in the light of the kingdom of God, and it is carried out by a changing church in an ever-changing world. Thus we are led to concur with the claim of a large body of Christians who in 1980 declared that:

> *"One that is conscious of the kingdom will be concerned for liberation, not oppression; justice, not exploitation; fullness, not deprivation; freedom, not slavery; health, not disease; life, not death. No matter how the poor may be identified, this mission is for them."*[3]

In any attempt we make to understand and respond to the mission of God, we need to take very seriously the following words of Bonhoeffer: "There is no relation to men without a relation to God, and no relation to God without a relation to men, and it is only our relation to men and God."[4] Our relation to each other and to God in Jesus Christ is experienced chiefly (but not only) through the church, and we need to discuss the nature of the church before we suggest the modes of integration of mission and church.

## THE NATURE OF THE CHURCH

Even a casual acquaintance with the Bible confronts one with the stark realization that the church is a most difficult and complex community to define. The concept of church in the Old Testament hovers continuously within the tension of the exclusivist perceptions of the Jews as the people of God, God's elect, the "Qahal," on the one hand, and the unconditional sovereignty of God in calling whomever God wills, on the other. So, for example, Cyrus of Persia is accorded the same title which Israel, or Jacob, or a prophet, enjoys: Cyrus is the servant of Yahweh. How unthinkable in ordinary Jewish terms! Again, God's salvation is not only for the elect (as far as ethnicity is concerned), it is to extend to the ends of the earth, and the Jews are to be a "light to the nations." Where are the boundaries of the church in such situations, and what are its true frontiers?

In the New Testament we find a different type of tension at work, not so much between Jewish and non-Jewish considerations, as in Acts, Galatians, or Romans, but rather, between the proclamation of the Kingdom of God by Jesus and the proclamation of the Gospel of Jesus Christ by the Apostolic Church. Jesus preaches the kingdom, while Paul preaches Jesus. So the proclaimer becomes the proclaimed, and those who accept the Gospel by baptism are said to have put on Christ. Collectively they are called saints, or they are referred to as "the Body of Christ," or some other image is used. Seldom, if ever, is the church defined, or referred to, in institutional terms; hardly is it mentioned in terms of status or organizational arrangement; never is it a settled establishment. The missionary preoccupations of the Apostolic Age are undoubtedly the reason for this, but the difficult question remains about how exactly is the church to be defined. Our most authentic clue seems to lie in the direction of understanding the meaning of church in the Bible, and thereafter, in terms of the Spirit. It is the Spirit of God in the Old Testament who guides the prophets, who also guides Jesus in his ministry, and who also empowers the earliest witnesses of the risen Jesus to proclaim Him as the Christ of God. This enables Paul to adopt something of a definitive approach when he proclaims that as many as are led by the Spirit of God are indeed the children of God. So the doctrine of the church and the doctrine of the Spirit in the Bible seem to be inseparable, and the New Testament proclaims that wherever the Spirit of the Lord is there is freedom. That freedom is either unconditional and Spirit-filled, or else it is no freedom at all. So that just as God in Christ broke free from the shackles of Judaism, so, too, does the Spirit keep God's children free from ecclesiasticism, and institutional or cultural captivity. "Churchianity" is totally invalid.

Our historic Christian tradition has enabled us to affirm in our liturgies that we believe in One, Holy, Catholic and Apostolic Church. These four terms are usually referred to as the "marks" of the church. We shall have occasion to discuss various aspects of these four marks throughout the rest of this book. For purposes of our reflections here, however, we will assume that the first two marks - One and Holy - are indicative of our understanding of the origin of the church. They have their origins in the character of the God who has been disclosed to us chiefly in the experience of Israel and in the Christ-Event. There is only one God, who is the Sovereign Lord of creation, the God and parent of Our Lord Jesus Christ. That God is characterized by Holiness. The people of God, within the framework of the Church, are expected to reflect the character of that God who has called them into being. So the church is one and holy chiefly because of its vocation from that One God who is Holy. We acknowledge that these marks of unity and holiness for the church involve much more than is being suggested here, but we simply wish to register this elemental understanding in order to move on to the other two marks - "catholic" and "apostolic." These appear to be areas of grave contention and division; yet they are areas from which our understanding of the meaning of mission, as it relates to the church, can proceed in several different directions.

The notion of the church's catholicity has created untold pain and anguish among Christians who virtually have no other theological problems. Some actually renounce the recitation of any of the historic creeds of the church because this one word "catholic" becomes, for them, something of a stumbling-block. "Catholic" seems to spell out everything to which they are opposed in the depths of their faith. So they prefer the word "Universal" or "Christian," or to drop it entirely. It represents, for them, the core element of <u>protest</u> in historical Protestantism which must never be allowed to die, or to wax thin for lack of meaning. I wish to suggest, however, that if we were to understand Catholicity, not in terms of historical or denominational traditionalism, but rather in terms of the demands of the whole tradition of the faith of the Gospel to which every Christian must affirm allegiance through baptism, we might well be further along the way of setting ourselves free to deal with a much bigger problem for us as Christians. This problem has to do with the meaning of catholicity as it relates to those who consider themselves to be Christians but who choose to remain outside of the church. What is our basic understanding of the challenge from those who claim to be Christians but wish to have nothing more to do with the church? Put another way, how do we relate to the increasing phenomenon of churchless Christianity in the world? A closely related issue is that of our relationship with those who are Christians no more - the "no-more Christians." We shall have to deal with that later on.

The German theologian Wolfhart Pannenberg has helped us to think through the meaning and the nature of this problem of churchless Christianity in his book <u>The Church</u>. Our forefathers and foremothers have often reminded us: "nearer to church farther from God"; and they have sometimes cynically suggested that if one wishes to see God's face one should stay far away from the church. I have heard eminent church leaders admit that they have experienced much more of the forgiving love of God, and the meaning of true peace and wholeness, amongst people who have nothing whatever to do with the church. The falling away of church membership in parts of the Western world is not entirely due to the loss of faith in God, but rather to the loss of a vision of God in the church. No one can deny that every denominational quarrel and conflict, either within denominations or between denominations, has served to weaken the credibility of Christianity as proclaimed by the church. But some people's faith in God, and in the power of the Gospel, has been strengthened as a result of these tensions; they have opted for maintaining a non-denominational, non-institutional form of Christian existence.

Pannenberg claims that "Christians who have reservations about the life of the church are often more open and less pretentious about what it means to be a Christian than active members are."[5] He also suggests that with the increase in denominational division and the autonomy of economic, political, and social life over against religion, and with religious allegiance rapidly becoming a private matter, the nature of Christianity began to change. For example, the churches in their separate state lost their claims to universality; religion (Christianity) still continued to permeate society and culture; there was much more emphasis on Christian freedom and tolerance, and general civil liberty; the basic issue of human rights, resulting from the idea of Christian freedom, gave strength to the acceptance of freedom from sin through faith in Christ, and not through religious allegiance. Pannenberg states:

> *"The development of the idea that this had general applicability to all humanity as the foundation of a new, nonsectarian, common basis for life in society was itself dependent at the start of the modern period on legitimation in terms of the principles of the Christian tradition."*[6]

No denomination of the Christian church possessed the capacity to express within itself this struggle for Christian freedom, and so churchless Christians emerged. It is a modern form of Christianity which we all have to take very seriously, whether we actually affirm it or not. Somewhere along the line the rebuke of Jesus to his exclusivist friends seems to stick like a lump in our denominational throats: "He who does not gather with me scatters." Pannenberg comments:

> *"It is the misfortune of this modern form of Christianity - open, tolerant, freedom loving - that it has found no institutional form of its own but must depend for its survival on denominational churches."*[7]

What we are dealing with here is a certain degree of ambivalence which the churchless Christian must experience since there is no question about whether the Christian faith can exist without a community of faith. But what happens to the universality of the Gospel and the faith when the average member of that community is overwhelmingly constrained by a denominational consciousness? His/her theology is denominational, as well as his/her liturgy, spirituality, priorities for witness and service; even his/her concept of God. For although they do not actually say it, many Christians infer that God is absolutely the highest member of their own denomination, and that God can only be adequately worshipped in their preferred style. But do we not need to experience and express at the same time the universality of Christianity and the wholeness of the Gospel? And is not the Christian outside of the church better able to demonstrate the true meaning of catholicity than the church-member, who so actively confuses the whole truth of the Gospel with a narrow denominational outlook? What should church members do? Should they leave the church in an attempt to become more authentically Christian? Is this really possible? The fact is that the outside Christians are often as they are because, by our separated state and self-centeredness, we who are insiders have driven them to leave. We are, therefore, faced with a major task of reconciliation at a number of levels if we are to become the major sign and symbol of the unity of humankind which is inherent in our belief in God as the Lord of history. This can come about when our understanding of the church as community is not only proclaimed but practiced at all levels. Let us briefly identify some of the characteristics of this community called church before we examine the meaning of mission as that integrating focus for the church.

First, since the days of Karl Barth, renewed emphasis has been placed on the meaning of the word 'church' in terms of the Greek word "ekklesia." The stress was placed on the call: the church was the community of those who were called together, out of the world, up to the life of God through the Word in the Bible. Perhaps the time has come for us to make a shift of emphasis away from the call as such, since this has always characterizes God's activity, and since there are so many ways in which God calls even those who are not within the fold of the visible church. We might well be on a better track if we were to think of the church more in terms of a community of response, a community which has accepted a new and special relationship with God through Christ, resulting from his own life of a radically obedient response to God. The notion of response does indeed presuppose a call, but it places more emphasis on the fact that the call could have been ignored, just as Jesus could have done. For if Jesus was not free to ignore the call of his Father, then everything goes wrong with the nature of his obedience "even unto death." The responsive community does not take the initiative away from God; what it does is to affirm continuously that ours is a decisive response to what has been offered to us through Jesus Christ. It also means that the nature of the call is just as continuous as the nature of the response.

Second, the church is eminently the community of the risen Christ, for there can be no Christian faith without faith in the fact that God raised Jesus from the dead. It is the life of the risen Christ which permeates the life of the church. Our understanding of the life of the Spirit of God is vacuous if we attempt to isolate the meaning of the resurrection either from the meaning of the Holy Spirit or from the essential nature of the church itself.

Third, the church is the community of forgiveness. This cardinal aspect of the nature of the church is very often missed because we are tempted to gloss over the reality of sin in our modern world. The ancient people of Israel grappled continuously with what was meant by the relationship that ought to exist between themselves and their God. They accustomed themselves to the use of the sacrificial system which did for them something of a patchwork job; but it never removed the guilt or the scar which sin had created. So total forgiveness was always an impossible experience for them. In the life, death and resurrection of Christ, Christians have come to an experience of that something extra which the sacrificial system of the Jews never afforded. So Christians know what it is to say that their sins have been forgiven by God; they also know what it is to be responsible for the proclamation and practice of the Gospel of forgiveness. Forgiveness means restoration. Wherever there is brokenness, there too must exist the possibility for restoration of relationships and structures. We must never forget that the first command which the risen Christ gave to the church in the upper room was to forgive the sins of others. This was the direct result of the peace, the "shalom," which He breathed into their presence. In the final analysis it is only those who truly know what it means to have been forgiven by God who can share in the ministry of forgiving others. This is the inescapable duty of the Christian fellowship. Furthermore, where there are modern manifestations of sin, there too must be activated the church's witness to the modern manifestations of God's forgiveness.

Fourth, the church is the community of transformation. No other aspect of human existence receives as much prominence in the message of the New Testament as the reality of God's transforming activity in Jesus Christ. Jesus, as the new Adam, or even as the New Moses, represents the radically new beginning which God has ushered into human affairs. Love becomes transforming love; truth becomes transforming truth; the kingdom of God comes with power, not in the overthrow of secular authority, but in the transformation of the real meaning of power. So Jesus makes a bold statement to remind Pilate that he could have no power at all unless he had derived it "from above." The church then as the community of transformation is both the <u>transformed</u> community as well as the <u>transforming</u> community. Within it the ordinary terms of reference are changed into extraordinary significance, and all of human life itself becomes sacred.

Fifth, the nature of community itself provides the church with a basic understanding of what are its prior obligations to its own members. A community is an order of sharing, a common order, an arrangement of mutuality, a fellowship of inter-accountability. A Christian is by definition one who shares; for the true value of the many blessings he/she has received from God cannot be affirmed unless he/she shares what God has given to him/her. The love of God means nothing to us unless we are actively engaged in giving it away. The reality of sharing then is crucial to our witness as Christians. Although Christianity is a personal religion, it is not to be an individualistic religion, but simply a religion of the person. It is impossible to overstress how important this virtue of sharing is for the church of today when there are so many variations on the theme of collective individualism within denominations. These have significantly exacerbated the problems experienced in the search for Christian unity. These words of Philip Potter may sound very harsh but they are very true:

> *"There is far too little sharing within and between the churches themselves - the sharing not only of material and technical resources which so much dominate our thinking, but all the gifts of grace that we have received. What we have learned in the ecumenical movement is that our disunity as churches is in large measure due to our incapacity to display this genuine sharing of gifts in love with one another. We tend too much to hang on to the inherited selfish forms of power and prestige, and above all the petrifying habit of self-sufficiency and obsequious begging."*[8]

Sixth, we need to constantly recognize that the church is a community in pilgrimage; it is a band of people on the way. The fundamental aspect of the church as a movement creates innumerable difficulties for the proper understanding of what is our real obligation as missionaries; for we find ourselves unable to overcome the feeling that we are bound by an institution called church. Whenever we allow the static feeling of the institution to overwhelm the dynamic consciousness of the movement or pilgrimage, things seem to go wrong. The prophet in us turns into the priest of the establishment; the fresh charism from God becomes the office; love becomes routine;

all our spirit-filled credentials are deflated by a preoccupation with the politics of preservation. While we can in no way pretend that we are living in New Testament times with all the pioneering fervor we sense from the literature of that era, we still need to acknowledge that the church cannot be true to itself if it is bound by anything other than the Kingdom of God. As a community in pilgrimage, the church is to be much less a sanctuary of tradition and much more a sign of the Kingdom. This means that it is marked by provisionality at every point, rather than by a sense of worldly permanence. It means that it is a society of anticipation, working and waiting for that which is still to come. There is so much of a not-yet-ness about the church that we should always have great difficulty in trying to determine what should be regarded as fixed, except the loving presence of God, which is God's grace. We are beings who live towards God's future.

What about the apostolicity of the church then? Is this to do with the origins of the church, especially where we seek to underline the apostolic tradition? Does the claim to be apostolic mean that we stand in line with what the first apostles believed and practiced? Is it the affirmation of a pristine nature, or even the exercise of apostolic authority - whatever that may mean? Apostolicity seems to me to have everything to do with why and how we have become Christians in the first place. Jurgen Moltmann in his book, The Church In The Power Of The Spirit, makes the claim that the four marks of the church - one, holy, catholic, apostolic - are not only statements of faith and hope, but they also are statements of action. He identifies unity with freedom, apostolicity with partisanship for the oppressed, and holiness with poverty. With respect to catholicity as universalism, Moltmann explains the Christian option for the oppressed with these words:

> *"The rich and the mighty are not rejected out of revenge but in order to save them. Masters are rejected because of their oppression, so that they may experience the fullness of common humanity, of which they are depriving themselves and others. Christian universalism will therefore be realized in particular conflict situations in a partisanship of this kind; otherwise it is still in danger of being abstract and of dissolving the community itself."*[9]

He speaks of apostolicity as "the church's special historical designation," and calls it a "designation of the kingdom." He says that the term apostolic denotes both the church's foundation and its commission.

Moltmann thus calls on the church, not so much to seek legitimation in its apostolic identity, but to do the equivalent of what the first apostolate was about, namely, to be oriented towards the future - the future of Christ. He says that the real apostolic church will leap forward to what is new and surprising because it will seek to fulfill Christ's apostolic mission in its own historical situation. Moltmann, therefore, perceives of apostolicity in the light of the crucified and risen Christ and suggests that participation in the mission of Christ -

> "... leads inescapably into tribulation, contradiction and suffering. The apostolate is carried out in the weakness and the poverty of Christ, not through force or the strategies of force. Reserved and withdrawn men and women and closed societies are opened through the witness of apostolic suffering, and can only through this be converted to the future of the kingdom."[10]

Pannenberg also places his thoughts on the eschatological grid when he states thus:

> "The apostolic doctrine is not expressed through traditional formulations as such, but only through the proclamation of the finality of the message and work of Jesus, proclamation always related to the present day and always casting light on the present experience, as it sets forth the message and work of Jesus as the truth that brings this unfulfilled world towards fulfillment. When it does this, the universal mission of the church is in one way or another a part of the apostolicity of the church."[11]

Both of these theologians are obviously right in their attempt to lift apostolicity into the vision of the future. But, nevertheless, there seems to be something special about the apostolic community called church which takes into account many other things: the compelling witness to the risen Christ in the faith of the whole church, the transforming power of the whole Gospel, the nature of the hope of the poor, the relentless surge of deep joy from those who seek to realize God's reconciling and healing love. All this seems to me to be also involved in apostolicity, not as an afterthought or secondary effect, but as fundamental reality. Time and again those who go forward because they are on a mission for Christ experience the joy and the depth of transformation as they actually go. The lepers - *"As they went they were cleansed."* The disciples - *"We saw Satan fall like lightening from heaven."* The Emmaus companions - *"Did not our hearts burn within us?"* Peter - *"I perceive that God is no respecter of persons."* So apostolicity seems to point not only to the foundations of the church, and to its commitment towards the future, but also to that unspeakable depth of being which the community of faith can only experience when it is actually on the mission road. The apostolic nature of the church is both mystical and missionary; we would, therefore, do well to discuss the integration of mission and church in this light.

## THE INTEGRATION OF MISSION AND CHURCH

If all that we have been saying so far about mission and the church is to be taken into account, what happens to the so-called mission of the church? Is the church merely a part of the mission, or is it the chief executing agency of that mission? Or, is the mission a much broader and deeper activity than the church community could ever seek to contain? We need to bear in mind certain factors of ambivalence which characterize our religious perspectives. First, God is active in history, in the world's history, outside of the church; and yet, the church sees itself as having a primary obligation to the world in God's name. Second, there is the continuing tension in the church between the sense of that which already is and that which is not yet. Third, the church as community feels the need for order, institutional arrangement, and lasting establishment; and yet, none of this actually bears out the essentials of what it is called to do. Fourth, although we are free from the assumption that God will always be on our side, whatever we do, we are never to arrogantly assume that we are always on God's side. Fifth, because of our human limitation and sin, the church is at one and the same time a sign of the Kingdom, and also a sign of what the Kingdom is not. Finally, whether as individuals or as groups, we find ourselves constantly caught within the tension of our legitimate quest for survival and prosperity (enjoying the good things which we say that God has provided for our use), and the need to travel lightly, because we have here no abiding city. Is the mission of God then concerned with us, or is it concerned with others? I would safely say that it is primarily concerned with the otherness of ourselves, and this is why, and how, mission and church can be integrated.

This focus on the otherness of ourselves will always be based on the realization that the only reality which we possess is our utter and complete dependence on God, who is the sovereign Lord of history. This means, in effect, that mission would have very little to do with either church growth or denominational spread. The struggle of the Christians to grow in grace is radically different from the struggle of any group of Christians to grow fatter. Indeed the one is antithetical to the other. The mission of God provides the stimulus for the church, not in going out to seek more members, but in keeping it actively engaged in the unfinished task of witnessing to the Kingdom of God. It is that which sustains the church in the value of hope in things not seen, rather than holding on to the many things which are seen but are not worth hoping for. If only we could see mission as the focal point of God's involvement in history, then the church would always be recognized as being the chief agency offering to the world faith, hope and love, not on its own account but on God's; and witnessing through faithful hope-in-action, in loyal response to what God has already done in the world. J. G. Davies is correct when he suggests: "the true goal of mission is not just to add a religious dimension to natural life but to be its true self as communion with God."[12] David Bosch adds yet another dimension to our understanding when he states thus:

> *"Mission takes place where the Church, in her total involvement with the world and the comprehensiveness of her message, bears her testimony in word and deed in the form of a servant, with reference to unbelief,*

> *exploitation, discrimination and violence, but also with reference to salvation, healing, liberation, reconciliation and righteousness."*[13]

We also need to keep before our minds the centrality of the Cross as the axis for mission. It was not for little, or for nothing, that Paul held firmly to his slogan: *"We preach Jesus Christ, and him crucified."* The writer of the letter to the Hebrews would further remind us that Jesus was crucified *"outside the gate."* Our testimony to the Crucified One must always be borne in the process of going out and away from our accustomed selves. The meaning of mission is very closely bound up with all of this, and we do well to underline these words of Simon Barrington-Ward:

> *"Once the church participates more fully in the death and risen life of its Head, that whole work of witness, in word, deed and being, which is mission, becomes, as in the New Testament church, more of a gift exchange, set in a context of friendship and genuine caring. Then it can be seen that Christ on his cross indeed grapples with the issues confronting all human beings and societies and their shifting faiths and cultures now as then. The truest exponents of mission are people in the Spirit committed, with Christ, to this grappling, people profoundly grasped by his divinely sharp yet wounded love, which is fully 'in the world' but yet never of it."*[14]

Bosch states quite profoundly:

> *"Mission never takes place in self-confidence but in the knowledge of our weakness, where danger and opportunity meet."*[15]

The integration of mission and church then is only possible in the living witness of the people of God who seek to resolve the inevitable tension between the world order and the church's self-understanding in the light of the faith that God raised Jesus from the dead, and that new life in Christ summons all to constant renewal and to fullness of life. Let us explore some of the implications which follow from this.

The integration of mission and church involves both a concern for "out-reach" as well as for "in-reach." The out-reach denotes not merely affirmation of the otherness of ourselves as Christians, but also the conscious provisionality which the responsive nature of our community demands. In-reach, then, is not to be seen as antithetical to out-reach; but rather, as the gradual realization of what we are called to do and to become. We find our true selves in Christ and his world as we reach out in faithful response to what God has already done in Christ.

We need to recognize the church less in terms of organization, or order, or establishment, and more in terms of its sacramental origin and nature. It is not that the church is a member of us ourselves functioning in service of our personal dreams or our social and political aspirations - however legitimate they might happen to be. Rather, we are fully members of the church which is a mystical community, and we bear in our lives its sacramental dimensions which are both visible and invisible. James White has pointed us to the significance of the sacramental life as persistence and continuity. Because the Christian is constantly surrounded by the realities of injustice, the struggle for justice is never an optional extra in Christian witness; it remains central. White writes thus:

> *"Because Christians experience God's self-giving in the sacraments, they can give themselves for others. The Church's contribution to social justice derives largely from its power of making God's love visible in the world through the sacraments. That visibility is a constant need for any Christian's lifelong growth, shaped and transformed by God's acts. Persistence is essential for efforts of justice ... the powers of evil are too strong, the rewards for wrong too lucrative to readily concede to single setbacks. Injustice is persistent, too, and only yields to greater persistence. The sacraments provide strong rations to enable Christians to 'hang in there' in the combat with evil."*[16]

Even if we would perhaps recoil from speaking of the sacraments in terms of "rations," we would however agree with White in respect of God's self-giving love and the meaning of persistence through the sacramentality of the Christian life. Church, mission, and sacrament seem to me to coinhere within the framework of God's gift to us. They draw heavily on each other for their meaning and significance.

White says that "sacraments set us free from obsession with self so we can give of ourselves."[17] This is particularly true of Baptism and the Eucharist, the two sacraments that must be understood in terms of mission, and which are at the same time central to the life of the church. By Baptism we are included in the obedience of Christ and his mission, and in the Eucharist our commitment to God and to God's mission is renewed. White has more to say about the Eucharist. He says it -

> *"... is both a source of power for the Christian to change society and a condemnation of false confidence in any existing society inasmuch as it falls short of that Kingdom God wills to bring about. The eucharist promises a much more radical vision for humanity than any social reformer has hoped to bring about through the dictatorship of the proletariat, laisser-faire capitalism, or any other purely human panacea."*[18]

In this connection we must not be unmindful of the divine ascendancy of the power of love over the human propensity for the love of power. The Eucharist plays no part in the latter. Mission itself is to bear testimony to the former.

There is undoubtedly an integral connection between mission and worship. But what is this connection? Some Christians readily make clear what they consider the distinction to be - namely, that mission is anthropocentric and emphasizes the horizontal dimension of the church's witness, while worship is theocentric and emphasizes the vertical dimension of that witness. While there is some value in such a distinction, there would seem to be greater value in affirming the meaning of mission and worship in terms of God's activity and human response. Mission and worship would therefore be acknowledged as interdependent functions, or aspects, of a single divine-human activity - God's enlisting of the human response to God's approach to humanity. Worship is thus offered to God on behalf of the whole human order; and engagement in the missionary enterprise is essentially the existential discovery of what baptism as faith-response both means and entails.

Contemporary missiologists are given to underlining the significance of the church's missionary intention. The thought behind this is that the expansionist design of particular Christian bodies need not, in this age of contexualization, be confused with or programmed into, the inherent characteristics the church's witness. Whether or not the "intention" can be pursued, the "dimension" still needs to be promoted. Perhaps the promotion of worship as mission, and mission as worship, might be the most appropriate means of liberating our attitudes from the dilemma of dimension versus intention. The over-riding intention of responding to God in all, and through all, that we can see God to be, renders the church's dimension of mission and worship neither separable nor incomplete.

Christian witness to the world is always conditioned by Christian witness in the world. No historical study of Christian missionary enterprise could dare ignore the fact that those who "carried the Gospel" to far-off lands often confused those who were to be "converted," because they were often in such bitter competition with their missionary counterparts. For example, the darker side of the emergence and growth of the Church of South India, or of the Church of North India, would betray the uncomfortable answer to the question of why there were so many different Christian churches in India. It has its origins in the basic human failure among Christians to strive to give expression to that unity which the Spirit has already given.

The Christians' mission to each other, as Christians, is no less important than that to non-Christians. It is difficult to perceive of a more effective sign of the meaning of Christian unity than that of experiencing the mutuality of affirmation and responsibility amongst Christians themselves.

A very strange corollary to this thought exists in the patent reluctance of some North American churchpersons to extend genuinely warm and open fellowship to churchpersons from the Third World. They often stop at nurturing a strong and proud delight in their provision of money and other resources for missionary enterprises in the Third World. Third World Christians often exclaim: "These people prefer to see us in pictures than to see us in person!" Is there a way out of this phenomenon, so strange and yet so true? Can mission and church be integrated on this point?

Like all other religions, Christianity is concerned with the relentless search for meaning in the world of human experience. The particularly Christian search is shaped by an unfolding understanding of the Gospel of Jesus Christ. The search is both intellectual and spiritual. While theologians and church leaders do much to promote the intellectual search, the obvious needs of the spiritual search often seem to be neglected. Why is the Christian witness in South Africa, or Russia, or Latin America spoken of today with such fervor and admiration? The answer seems to lie in the fact that the Christians there have been forced to integrate the meaning of mission and church through the experience of a common responsive and interpretive spirituality. Black South African Christians have known what it means to practice the "spirituality of liberation" in the face of the most powerful regime in their history. Constitutional racism in Pretoria, plus Western support, ranked second to none in terms of effective control of blacks. Even American presidents are forced to resign under the pressure of "national pride." But that same "pride" ensured the viability of a racist South African regime for a generation. Yet, God seems to provide God's own with an appropriate spirituality in the context of this and every other situation. Such a spirituality offers a provisional answer to their persistent question: Whose side is God on?

One must not ignore the difficulties involved in discovering what are the divinely authentic elements of an interpretive spirituality. The former South African regime had historically based itself and its policies on a spirituality which its proponents believed to have been made in heaven. Pannenberg calls for a renewed connection between sanctification and politics. He writes:

> *"The political impact of a Christian theory of justice will depend upon the renewal of the theocratic idea; and a spiritual theocracy can be effective only through a theory of justice that uses the theocratic framework in redefining social reality."*[19]

There is much in this statement with which one would, on the face of it, be forced to disagree. Nevertheless, the need for an interpretive spirituality is important for the cause of 'redefining social reality.' Let it also be said that the Christian is pre-occupied with meaning and faithful response, rather than with social reconstruction.

The Lutheran theologian, Carl E. Braaten, in his book, The Flaming Center, has called for the exorcism of some contemporary demons in order to make way for the universal gospel. Braaten lists the demons as follows:

    (a) a retreat to an historical mysticism in religion;
    (b) subjective experience as the norm of theology;
    (c) the retrenchment of church in society, seeking its own security behind a wall of separation;
    (d) a relapse into legalism and immorality, the placing of a precedence on law over the course of freedom;
    (e) a resurgence of nationalism in world affairs.[20]

Now, if one were to ask a Desmond Tutu, or a Fidel Castro, to list what they consider to be five contemporary 'demons,' one imagines that the list would differ in each case. It mainly depends on where you are, and the quality of vision you bring to your concerns. The cultural matrix is indispensable.

Braaten offers us a very curious piece of proclamation; and we need to refer to it in the light of our concern that the integration of mission and church should also take place in our identification of the demonic dimensions of our experience. He contends:

> *"The greatness of the Christian mission, despite its overwhelming attachment to Western culture, is that it has successfully started new churches in non-Western cultures. This is the best proof of the transcendent origins and universal validity of the Christian message."*[21]

The greatness and transcendence of the Gospel would seem to lie entirely in the opposite direction in its freedom from the demonic manipulation of, and 'attachment' to, any culture, starting with the Jewish, and in its universal capacity to shed quite easily the trappings by which it moves from one place to another. So that, on the whole, there is great theological merit is seeking to promote the inter-cultural over the cultural mode of communicating the Gospel. There is the inherent duty of the Christian to witness against the demonic "absolutizing" of the Gospel in any culture or presumed super-culture. The Kingdom of God is supra-cultural.

We often speak of the prophetic mission of the church; and by that we seem to imply the obligation on the part of the few to be aggressive, outspoken, daring, confrontational, or even eccentric. All of these attitudes may indeed have their place and exemplars. But what does being prophetic mean in the light of the ministry and mission of Jesus of Nazareth? To what extent is the proclamation of the Gospel bound up with the response to a prophetic vocation? Who shares in that vocation, and who does not? To whom is the prophet sent? By whom? When does the particular prophetic role cease? Is it institutional? Or, indeed, can it ever be an institutional role? Could Saul be truly leader of Israel, and prophet in Israel at the same time? Or is prophecy an inherent dimension of religious leadership? The concept of Christian prophecy is fraught with some grave difficulties. It is no wonder that the early Church seemed eager to usher such an office into early insignificance. The office goes but the vocation still remains, however, vague and indeterminate.

The Church is called to be in itself a prophetic minority to the world on God's behalf. It is called to take the risk of proffering and living in critical reflection and response to the world in the light of the unfolding Word of God. It is associated with bad news when it fails to respond faithfully to the cross-bearing demands of the Gospel of Jesus Christ. Its motivation is God's revelation, God's self-disclosure. Its medium is Christological - the proclamation and practice of the Lordship of Christ in history, over against Christ's Lordship of history. The implications of this distinction are enormous, but would carry us far beyond the scope of this discussion. Its message is to be found in the proleptic interpretations of history - every time is God's time, and the future is there already, but it is still on the way. The prophetic integration of mission and church lies in the dynamic conjunction of ultimate concern with present reality. There is no alternative.

The question of an appropriate Christian ethic is always a difficult one to propose, since the meaning of 'appropriate' is directly related to the particular situation. Be that as it may, we should still be able to posit a general ethical framework which ought to inform the Christian conscience towards right conduct. Ethicists are not always clear on what are the elemental constructs of virtue, or on what method of co-identification should be applied to the so-called cardinal virtues and the Christian virtues. It would seem incumbent on the Christian, however, that the virtue of love should be accorded a pivotal place in our understanding of right conduct. Love carries with it some basic characteristics in the light of the Gospel, and because of the revealed character of God. It not only signifies radical renewal in the human experience, but it also denotes a process of sanctification in which the agency of God takes hold of the activity of humankind as a result of a radical renewal or regeneration.

This has implications for the question of ordinary human integrity. Human integrity is not necessarily Christian integrity - Jesus of Nazareth often alluded to this in his preaching. Something more always seemed to be required of the Christian. It is here, too, that mission and church must be seen to be integrated. The church must not merely stand for something, it should most certainly be seen to stand for something more. The ethic of ambivalence and vacillation is roundly condemned by Jesus. The ethic of sanctification knows nothing of two masters, or of double-mindedness, or of mixed and uncertain sounds. The vacillation is evident when Christians are merely church-oriented rather than mission-controlled. The former keep "God" in their hands and pockets; the latter worship God in their hearts - at the center of their lives. The ethic of sanctification and Christian integrity has its ramifications in the church's response to questions such as the sanctity of human life, nuclear weaponry and global peace, social justice, racism, sexism, and imperialism. They are not easily resolved; but they should not be readily evaded either.

Finally, there is still the issue of the relationship with those who "follow not with us." How does the integration of mission and church affect such a relationship? Who are these people anyway, and what are the priorities of their concerns? To what extent do they really differ from the church-member Christians? Some were born and reared in other religious traditions. Some were regular church-member Christians. But they have since chosen to become church-less Christians to pursue their own distinctive spirituality. Some were once Christians, but are now Christians no more; yet, they have not acquired for themselves any new labels. Some have never had any religious training or discipline at all, and have been reared in a totally secularist environment. What is the Christian attitude to such classes of people, many of whom may be our associates, colleagues, clients or relatives? Many of them present an embarrassing contrast to regular Christians by reason of their witness against human depravity and social sin.

Do we not need to pose the question from the standpoint of God's probable relationship with them? How does God view their Christ-like actions although they are not Christians? David Bosch contends:

> *"God looks more kindly on the indignation of those who rebel against injustice, hunger, exploitation and suffering than on those religious hucksters who preach a gospel of individualistic and hedonistic faith which shuns all controversy."*[22]

While it may not be possible to speak with certainty about God's comparative assessment, Bosch's comment is to be understood as an affirmation of the divine disfavor of social and human discomfort. But are we ascribing to God's judgement what we consider to be unacceptable to ourselves? Do we call pain and suffering evil simply because they are uncomfortable for us? Is pain evil in the sight of God? This is an ongoing philosophical and theological debate, but it is related to our present concern about God's approval of those persons and things of whom we, as regular Christians, would rather disapprove.

In conclusion, we must say that mission and church integrate at the point where we make the conscious decision not to "play God," but rather to obey God. As servants of the Kingdom, we give ourselves in faithful and loyal obedience to that vocation, and we witness with fervor and love to what we have received from God. We testify in loving and sanctifying relationships with others (however different they may be in faith or style), for God is able to relate to them in God's own way. Thus, our attitude to mission is that we will always be ready to proclaim, while being always ready to learn. Ours is the responsibility to enlist ourselves with others in the cause of human rights and social justice, so long as our faith assures us that this is in faithful response to the Gospel. "Not-yet-Christians" and "no-more-Christians" may well be active participants in God's total mission in a way that is not readily clear to us. It is more dangerous for God's mission and the church if we opt for cautious withdrawal rather than risk positive engagement. After all, what do we wish for ourselves that we would not wish for them? The church for the mission is the community of the Spirit, always risking the Gospel on the new frontiers of God's world. We are an unfolding living parable of God's Kingdom. We need to struggle to become who we are.

To be in mission is always to be involved not only in proclaiming the Gospel, but also in reclaiming it. To reclaim the Gospel calls for a new sense of eschatology, a new sense of the dawn of the end-times, the in-breaking of that which is radically new. The true Christian functions on the borders of the wilderness, on the borders of change, in full anticipation of a new Canaan. There is always the memory of what lies on the border on the other side of the wilderness - the Egypt from which we are being emancipated. Returning to Egypt should not be an option for the Christian. Yet the church should never create either an Egypt-like climate or a wilderness form of existence for any of its members. In our next chapter, therefore, we shall relate the experiences of three early Caribbean Afro-Anglicans who sought to function on the borders of the wilderness within the established church in America, but who found no support for the change and freedoms to which their sense of mission from God had directed them.

## CHAPTER FOUR

## *HONESTY WITHIN – PROPHETS WITHOUT*

The official photograph of Anglican bishops assembled for the 1988 Lambeth Conference gives the casual observer one very significant piece of information. It shows that Ecclesia Anglicana, the world-wide Anglican Communion, is now much more a non-white global communion of churches than ever before, and that the number of non-Caucasian, non-European bishops is clearly in the ascendancy. On a global scale, the once typical white male Anglican bishop, with English as his first language, is now a minority, and the likelihood of the Anglican Church remaining as a global bastion, symbolic of the historical vestiges of British imperialism, is now on the decline.

Times are changing fast, and so is the Anglican Communion, which, like the former British Empire, once boasted that it was the earthly realm on which the sun never set. Anglicanism went out from England with the colonial and mercantile expansionists, and it was originally designed to embellish the grand aspirations of white European domination and control, which the British understood to be their genetic heritage and divine birth-right. Plantation colonies relied heavily on the exigencies of the Anglican Church to provide the necessary instruments of social containment and civilizing tendencies, sufficient enough to induce the working classes towards better forms of subordination, cooperation, and productive labor. This was particularly the case in the British West Indies, where the Anglican Church held sway over the social institutions, while it enjoyed a position of privilege as the church of the British Crown.

The face of Anglicanism in the West Indian colonies at the end of the last century was thus vastly different from the face of Anglicanism in the Lambeth Conference photographs of that day. The teeming masses of Afro-Caribbeans filled the ranks of the West Indian congregations, even if they were mostly led by white clergymen from the Mother Country. What was there to which brilliant and enterprising Afro-Caribbeans could aspire? How could they interpret their moral duty and social status in such a denominational environment? Where would their primary loyalties lie? How would they give pride of place to their blackness, their African heritage, when the Church to which they belonged regarded their presumed ethnic inferiority as a divinely ordered fact? Were they Africans first, or Anglicans? Many of them would have sung:

> *The rich man in his castle,*
> *The poor man at his gate,*
> *God made them high and lowly,*
> *And ordered their estate.*

Such words were familiar to them from one of their well-known hymns which began with these words:

> *All things bright and beautiful,*
> *All creatures great and small,*
> *All things wise and wonderful,*
> *The Lord God made them all.*

However much Afro-Caribbeans strove to acquire the intellectual competencies or social graces of their British leaders, they still realized that they could never become their equals, unless they were born again in different climes and from different genes. Historically, just as white Methodism in America gave rise to the need for Black Methodism, so colonial Anglicanism gave rise to the need for Afro-Anglicanism. Afro-Anglicanism is the authentic attempt to interpret and respond to the Gospel of Jesus Christ, while remaining Anglican by religious persuasion, and African by ethnic and cultural heritage at the same time. Sometimes it worked, sometimes it did not. This chapter is, therefore, about the story of three West Indian clergymen during the latter decades of the last, and the early decades of this century, whose attempts to be fully Anglican and African at the same time were conspicuously frustrated, and who thus turned themselves into significantly historic personalities who tried to be honest within the church, but who had to find their prophetic axis outside. These men were: Joseph Robert Love (Bahamas), George Alexander McGuire (Antigua), and Reginald Grant Barrow (Barbados).

How did these men navigate their way through the turbulent waters of their church; and how did they happen to end up as ex-Anglican clerics? Each of their Afro-Anglican stories makes for very illuminating insight about some early efforts at Afro-Evangelism. Afro-Anglicans played a very prominent role in the development of Afro-Evangelism at the turn of this century. It was their determination to link their African heritage and their understanding of the Gospel to the cause of advancement for their fellow-blacks, and to place it significantly above their minimal Anglican privileges, which marked them out as signal characters in a still unfolding story of black religion struggling to find its fullness in a white-dominated society. It is in such a context that the West Indies and the United States of America have shared so very much in a common history.

## JOSEPH ROBERT LOVE

Joseph Robert Love was born in Nassau, Bahamas, in 1839. His parents were full-blooded African, and there can be no doubt that Love's blackness meant very much to him throughout his entire life. His early education and religious influences were mainly guided by the work of two Anglican priests, William Woodcock and J. Hartman Fisher, who were rectors of St. Agnes Church. St. Agnes Church has historically been the largest Anglican congregation in Nassau, comprised mainly of the lower classes of Afro-Bahamians who live "over the hill." This epithet is a Bahamian expression related to the demographic geography of Nassau, indicating that on the other side of the hill in the city the whites and the wealthy could be found. They attended other churches, including the Cathedral.

Love attended the Mico School in Nassau, having been sponsored by another Anglican cleric, Archdeacon J.M. Trew. Trew's reputation for championing the cause of blacks in Jamaica and the Bahamas was very well-known. There can certainly be no doubt that Love held Trew in very high esteem, and he often referred to Trew's high principled forthrightness which he faithfully tried to emulate. He became a teacher and a lay-reader in the Anglican Church, and made a very good impression from the start as a public orator. This talent of persuasive oratory was to be of incalculable importance not only for Love, but also for the other two persons we shall be discussing later.

Whether or not the Anglican Church can take much credit for this is very debatable since many speaking opportunities in Anglican churches were not available to blacks throughout the West Indies. This gave cause for the rise of many sectarian congregations among the more enterprising West Indian religious leaders who knew that they had something better to say than what they had heard in Anglican conventicles. Perhaps more credit must be given to the British influence on West Indian education, and to the enforced cultural need to "speak properly" (like the British) in order to be acceptable, coupled with local familiarity with the Book of Common Prayer, Hymns: Ancient And Modern and the literary appeal of William Shakespeare and poets, made popular by frequent recitations and public oratory in the dominant local culture. Whatever it was, Love mastered the English language at an early age, and his work as teacher and religious leader afforded him the opportunity to advance his skills.

The lack of opportunities for advancement in the Bahamas, coupled with the recruitment of black West Indian men to serve as priests in black Episcopalian congregations in the United States during the 1860's, seemed to have been the major drive behind Love's move to America. There were also some infelicities in his social behavior which created something of a cloud over his character. He was trained at a Seminary in Philadelphia for the priesthood between 1865 and 1869, and was eventually ordained deacon early in 1871. He was the first black to be ordained in the Diocese of Florida. His work in Jacksonville included running a school for colored children sponsored by the Commission of Home Missions for Colored People.

From Jacksonville he quickly moved to Savannah, Georgia, becoming again the first black to be appointed a rector in that Diocese, at St. Stephen's Church. Within a year, he moved again, and established his own St. Augustine's mission chiefly for dark-skinned members, since the members of St. Stephen's, who were of lighter hue, found it impossible to follow Love's urging to bring darker-skinned Episcopalians into the full life and governance of the congregation. By June 1876, he had moved to St. Phillip's, Buffalo, where for the next five years, according to Love, he was to spend the happiest days of his life, first as rector and then as a medical student at the University of Buffalo. He was thus the first black to graduate from that University.

It was during this period that he was also ordained priest, and committed himself to missionary work in Haiti both as a priest and a doctor, under the leadership of Bishop Theodore Holly. Love was greatly impressed by the mind and work of Bishop Henry McNeal Turner of the AME Church; but the plight of the negroes in America did not provide for him as strong a challenge as the plight of the blacks in Haiti. He had long been a strong admirer of the great Haitian revolutionary Toussaint L'Ouverture. He described his commitment to the work in Haiti in this way:

> *"I have studied and taken my degree in Medicine in preparation for this special work, and from the firm conviction that the 'gift of healing' will enable me more effectually to reach all classes of my people through 'that touch of nature which makes the whole world kin' ... I mean to identify myself with this people, in national life and interests, as I already am in the race, to dwell with them, to die among them, and to be buried in their midst, if God permits."*[1]

Love therefore moved to Port-au-Prince, Haiti, in 1881, to begin his period of turbulent involvement in the religious and social affairs of that country. Within six months he was in trouble with Holly, and by September 1883 he was deposed from the Episcopal ministry, after a trial in the ecclesiastical court. Thereafter, he entered more fully into the socio-political life of Haiti, making his living as a medical practitioner, and holding tenaciously to his rights as a British subject in a foreign country. But his writings and other public pronouncements continued to bring him into trouble with the local political establishment, and he was eventually expelled for a second time to Jamaica in June 1890. It was to be in Jamaica that Love's major contribution to Afro-Evangelism was to burst forth, and where he was to have a crucial influence on the lives of many black Jamaicans, among whom was Marcus Mosiah Garvey.

Love's possible career as an Anglican priest in the Bahamas had ended with his move to America. His work as an Episcopal priest in Buffalo was rapidly followed by his embarking on a medical/missionary career in Haiti. His career as an Episcopal priest in Haiti was short-lived, and his eventual expulsion to, and resettlement in, Jamaica was as a political activist, rather than as a clergyman. Yet he never left the Anglican Church, as he had vowed never to do. He wrote in a letter to Holly in 1881: "But out of the Anglican Communion I will never go. I was born in her, baptized, confirmed, educated and ordained by her and by God's help, I will allow no earthly power to prevent my dying in her."[2] Indeed, one of his most prominent publications was a blistering attack on Roman Catholicism which he entitled, Romanism Not Christianity, published in 1892.

Between 1890, and his death in 1914, Love functioned as a leader of social and political thought in Jamaica, through his involvement in electoral politics as an elected member of the Legislative Council, in the production of newspapers, mainly The Jamaica Advocate, and through his active support of social organizations run by blacks, or for the support of blacks. It was written of him that he was "the first public figure [in Jamaica] to challenge the tacit assumption that blackness and inferiority were synonymous."[3] Dr. Joyce Lumsden's considered opinion of Love is that his "attachment to the Church of England existed pari passu with his belief in the superiority of the British law and constitution to any other system he knew."[4] This attachment was reinforced by his sojourn in the United States and Haiti. Thus his strong support for the British ethos and his equally strong commitment to the advancement of the African race not only constituted a major historical ambiguity, but also provides us with a unique story for the study of early Afro-Evangelism from an Afro-Anglican prophetic exile.

What then was Love's message? We may best sum it up in the following points. One, he brought the issue of blackness, as a skin-color, into the full public debate in Jamaica. He had said of himself: "I think so much of my beautiful black skin."[5] However, there was to be no narrowness of thought or attitude. He made clear his position with these words: "We love the white man because he is a BROTHER; we love the coloured man because he is a SON; we love the black man because we must love ourself. He whose sympathies are not as broad as that is something less than a man."[6] As far as Love was concerned, there was only one Race, the Human Race. His religious convictions enabled him to say: "I love all men and women whom God has been pleased to make."[7] He attacked the white establishment of his day not because it was white but simply because it discriminated against blacks, and therefore was subversive to the advancement of black rights and black dignity.

Two, he called on the Jamaican blacks to use their intelligence, their wit and honesty, in participating in the political process, especially in the use of their ballot, and in their rights to be elected to public office. He regarded it as the greatest offensive and defensive weapon they had to ensure that in voting they chose their equals and not their <u>masters</u>. This does not mean that Love supported black candidates because they were black. Indeed, Love held to the view that there were whites who could be counted on to genuinely support the black cause. Nevertheless, it could be said of him that his self-imposed task was to "make the men, and women, of his own race [color] alive to their obligations and opportunities, and in the political field he had achieved a fair measure of success."[8]

Three, he called on the blacks to do three basic things - Work, Save, and Educate. He held to the view that blacks in a British colony had the full rights and privileges under the constitution, born under the Union Jack, even though their antecedents were from West Africa. Thus blacks did not require any special methods or extraordinary means, for they could accomplish just as much as the Englishman. He once wrote: "Education, wealth and moral strength are what you are to seek to acquire and by these you will win your way to the first ranks, socially and politically."[9] There was absolutely nothing inherently inferior in the Negro, and he would fight to the end to so proclaim that Gospel. Listen to him:

> *"We have loved ... Englishmen all our life. We have considered ourselves so identified with them nationally as to be <u>one of them</u>. But if it is to be the doctrine of England (as it is of the United States) that the black man must be treated as an 'inferior' because the Caucasian race must be 'dominant' we will hate England and Englishmen as bitterly as we hate the United States and the negrophobists of that country. We could love no country, call no place 'home', feel proud of no nation where, and by whom, we are denied the equality of manhood."*[10]

Four, he took the meaning and practice of freedom very seriously indeed. For him, freedom was "the right and the power to develop social, civic and political manhood."[11] Such freedom involved thought, speech, and action; it also involved the freedom to organize for the pursuit of the highest goals of negro existence. One of his major contributions to Jamaican history therefore was to organize the People's Convention between 1898 and 1903. Queen Victoria's Diamond Jubilee in 1897 gave the stimulus for Love to suggest a diamond jubilee of Negro Emancipation from slavery in 1898. His efforts at rallying the blacks into an organization of their own were moderately successful. The objects of the People's Convention were as follows:

> *"... the development and perpetuation of the sense of obligation and responsibility in the emancipated people of this land; the assistance and guidance of the people in all matters relating to their moral, social and mental development and progress; the free discussion of all those questions affecting their vital interests, and the taking of such steps as will lead to the obtainment of all the advantages which belong to a free people."*[12]

Five, he was vigorously opposed to any philosophy or cultural initiatives which lessened the resolve of Jamaican blacks to assume the commanding heights of their European training, or a first-rate education. He was not in favor of a back-to-Africa movement, nor did he find himself in sympathy with Haitian Voudun, Jamaican obeah, or even popular Roman Catholic piety. These he found to be distractions to the major social task of full British citizenship both in Africa, for the Africans, and in Jamaica for the Jamaicans. Social and economic status was the goal, for Love could recognize that "the blue-eyed Saxon will clasp the hand of the blackest negro if it is lined with gold."[13]

Joseph Robert Love, a native Bahamian, made his indelible mark on Jamaican political and social history, and used his Afro-Anglican perspective, his African sensitivities, and his commitment to Afro-Evangelism to advance the cause of the poor and underprivileged masses in Jamaica. Although he did not function as a clergyman in Jamaica, his religious formation and involvement in social agonies of the United States and Haiti among blacks, helped to make him an Afro-Evangelist par excellence. His pulpit was the newspaper, the platform, and the Legislative Council; his sheep were the teeming masses in Jamaica yearning to be truly free; and the fruits of his labors were etched not in the stained glass windows but in the monumental strides with which Jamaican cultural and political life has affirmed the full social personhood of Jamaican blacks for the rest of this century. As an Afro-Anglican prophetic exile, he accomplished more than he could ever have done within the confines of Ecclesia Anglicana. Let us now turn to see what were the fruits of our second Afro-Anglican personality, George Alexander McGuire.

## *GEORGE ALEXANDER MCGUIRE*

Love was born in the Anglican Church and never left it; the Anglican Church left him. McGuire was born the son of an Anglican father and a Moravian mother, baptized an Anglican, grew up as a Moravian, trained as a Moravian pastor, confirmed as an Episcopalian in Philadelphia and later ordained, advanced through several positions in the Episcopal Church, and eventually left it to form his own church. McGuire is a very flambouyant character in the history of Black religion in this country, chiefly because of his work in the Episcopal Church, and his subsequent founding of the African Orthodox Church. Much has already been written about his fascinating life story, and I do not propose to repeat much of it here. Like myself, he was born on the island of Antigua, which, in my view, is still the "Gem of the Caribbean." He attempted to make a significant contribution to the life of the Anglican Church in this country, but his efforts were frustrated into his exodus. I would draw your attention to the work of The Rev. A. Terry-Thompson, Dr. Randall Burkett, Dr. Gavin White, Dr. Richard Newman, and more recently, that of my colleague Dr. Elias Farajaje-Jones. My chief point of focus here is to discuss McGuire's main concerns as an Afro-Anglican

Extract, and the forces which led to his becoming one. His contribution to our study of Afro-Evangelism is important, for it helps us to understand the difficulties experienced by an outstanding Black West Indian clergyman in his efforts to minister to his fellow-Blacks within the context of a white-dominated church, at the beginning of this century.

McGuire was born on March 26, 1866, in Sweets Village, Antigua, and after receiving the best possible education on the island, he went to a small Moravian Seminary in St. Thomas for training as a pastor. Following a period of six years ministry on the island of St. Croix, he moved on to the United States in 1894, was confirmed in 1895, made deacon in 1896, ordained priest in 1897. After a very active and energetic ministry in the Episcopal Church, and a five year stint back in Antigua (1913-1919), he was received into the Reformed Episcopal Church in October, 1919, formed the Independent Episcopal Church the following year, appointed Chaplain-General of the fledgling Universal Negro Improvement Association under Marcus Garvey the same year, whence he formed his own African Orthodox Church in 1921, after having being consecrated to the "Sacred Order of the Episcopate," by the notorious Archbishop Joseph Rene Vilatte of the American Catholic Church. It was said of him:

> *"So great was the desire for Ecclesiastical freedom because of the limitations and injustices as well as insults, that he resolved to cast off for ever the yoke of white Ecclesiastical dominance."*[14]

The story of the African Orthodox Church during and after the time of Patriarch McGuire is also a very fascinating one, and we shall pass it by for now, although we shall return to it briefly when we come to look at Barrow. My basic concern here is to explore McGuire's main thoughts through two important texts: His First Annual Missionary Report to the Bishop and Council of the Diocese of Arkansas in 1906, and his Speech in Liberty Hall New York, on August 1, 1924. It is important to remember, however, that McGuire was, like Love before him, a very eloquent cleric, widely read, medically trained, and deeply committed to the advancement of the Negro. His experience in the Episcopal Church was indelibly affected by his work in Arkansas, as Archdeacon for coloured work (1905-1908), (perhaps the highest possible appointment in the Episcopal Church open to a Black at that time), under the infamous Bishop William Montgomery Brown, and the refusal of the Church to grant independent status to the Black St. Bartholomew's congregation in Boston in 1911.

In his "First Annual Missionary Report" of 1906, Archdeacon McGuire was mainly concerned about promoting the argument in favor of Black suffragan bishops rather than Black missionary bishops, for work among Black Episcopalians. The stronger arguments among Blacks were in favor of missionary bishops, but this was not supported by the white Episcopalians with any enthusiasm. McGuire wanted to make a try for Black suffragans, even though he eventually changed his mind on this score. The central question had to do with what was the most appropriate and effective way of providing episcopal oversight for the ministry amongst Afro-Anglicans in the United States. Should they have bishops of their own race? McGuire suggested that "the most vexed problem of the American people is that which concerns the Afro-American. He is the storm-center around which rages our greatest controversies, whether in politics, religion, society or education. The American Church is being irresistibly drawn into the whirlpool."[15]

McGuire contended that the Episcopal Church was very unenthusiastic and lethargic in adapting to the needs of the Negro race, although Negroes were not lacking in their loyalty and love for the Episcopal Church. "The crucial hour is upon us... Will she rise supremely to the opportunity and duty of the hour, and considering racial differences, prejudices and peculiarities, relieve her Negro clergy and people of much embarrassment and supply them with the entire machinery for doing successful work among their own race without becoming schismatics, or asking for an autonomous 'ecclesiola in ecclesia?'"[16]

He referred to the two general objections to special Missionary jurisdictions. The first related to the difficulties involved in providing hospitality and entertainment for Black bishops. McGuire responded by saying that "The Church need give herself no uneasiness on this phase of the question. Negro churchmen are possessed of common sense. They respect their own feelings, as well as the customs and traditions of the land."[17] In other words, they would never go where they knew they were not particularly welcome; and in any case, said McGuire, "Negroes prefer to be entertained by Negroes, even as Whites by Whites."

The second related to what he called the "principle of ecclesiastical and diocesan territorial rights." McGuire made the very interesting point that the American Church had already violated its own principle at the parochial level anyway. He advanced the following observation:

> *What has become of the old law of parochial authority and jurisdiction? Has it not been rendered obsolete by the frequent erection of Negro parishes with Negro Rectors in towns, or portions of towns, in which there is already in existence a white parish with its rector? And in a larger way, are there not two Archdeacons in this very Diocese, appointed by the same Diocesan, whose fields are geographically identical, but each one confining his labors to the people of his own race?.... If we have Negro parishes operating within white parishes, and Negro convocations overlapping white convocations or Dioceses, does it seem a hard and radical thing to erect a Missionary Jurisdiction out of a Negro convocation, or several Negro convocations, and to place over such a Negro Bishop?*[18]

McGuire disclosed that Black Baptists and Methodists were contemptuous of

Black Episcopalians as people with a "black body with a white head," and that the only way self-respecting and intelligent Blacks would be attracted into the Episcopal Church was if they had bishops of their own race. "Negro clergy need loving, fraternal, and social intercourse with their Bishop," he said. He went on: "Receiving many considerations of kindness, official and personal, from my present Bishop, nevertheless, my manly dignity, my self-respect, my whole nature - intellectual, social and spiritual - yearns for a Bishop of my own race, who, besides giving me godly admonitions, will enter into my life as he alone can, and who is not prohibited from intermingling in every way, with me and the congregation commmitted to our charge."[19]

He had settled on the option for suffragan bishops, not because it was better than the missionary bishops' option, but because it was the least radical and less likely to arouse the antagonism of the diocesan bishops who, after all, were only human and would not readily concur with any jurisdictional incursions. He also agreed that the other Afro-American clergy strongly preferred the missionary option, radical though it was. Their strategy was: "We know what we want. Let us ask for that and nothing less, leaving it to the Church to give what she will."[20] It is important not to overlook this critical difference between McGuire's position at this point and that of his Afro-American colleagues among the clergy. It was perhaps indicative of a tension that existed, in one form or another, between West Indian clergy and their Afro-American counterparts, exacerbated mainly by socio-historical, cultural, educational, and political differences. It also pointed to the existence of the most complex perennial problem among Black leaders in America, namely, how do you deal effectively with the white man and the institutions under his control?

McGuire ended his report by asserting his determination to remain a member of the Anglican Church into which he was born, regardless of the outcome - "no legislation, nor lack of it, shall drive me from the Anglican Communion," he said. He went on: "We have race pride; and it is that which prompts us to ask for Negro Bishops. We care naught about social equality. But we do want the full development of our inherent capacity for constructive leadership, in secular as well as ecclesiastical matters where our own race is concerned."[21] McGuire failed in his bid to persuade the Diocese of Arkansas to take the idea of suffragan bishops seriously. He was in a worse predicament by serving under a bishop who had called for separate churches altogether for the Whites and the Negroes, mainly because he believed that the mixing of the races was perhaps the greatest social evil that America was experiencing. Brown believed that "a God-implanted race prejudice makes it impossible, absolutely so, that Afro-Americans and Anglo-Americans should ever occupy the same footing in a dual racial church."[22] We must never forget, however, that Bishop Brown was eventually declared a heretic and deposed in 1925.

McGuire did in fact go back on his word not to leave the Anglican Church. He tried to convince the Episcopal Church that its responsibility to the Negro was not an optional extra, but to no avail. In his capacity as Field Secretary for the American Church Institute for Negroes, McGuire wrote in his 1912 Report the following words:

"We do not owe the Negro what we have not, but we do owe the Negro the best that we have."[23] After his sojourn in Antigua, and his return to the United States, he found fresh impetus for the cause of the Negro in the new Marcus Garvey movement, which was being set up with headquarters in New York, and with which he enthusiastically joined in common cause. But the political complexities of non-governmental Negro organizations, particularly among West Indian immigrants always proved difficult, and McGuire found his strongest power-base in his own African Orthodox Church.

Our second document is his now famous sermon in New York's Liberty Hall, on West Indian Emancipation Day, August 1, 1924. The text of his sermon was taken from Exodus 4:2 *"And the Lord said unto him, What is that in thine hand? And he said, A rod."* It was delivered at the Fourth International Convention of the UNIA, where he was heralded as the Honorary Chaplain-General; he was presiding over the 'canonization' of Jesus as the Black Man of Sorrows. He began by exegeting the passage from which the text is taken, and waxed eloquent about the charge which Moses receives from God. The rod, he said, was a rod of authority, divinely consecrated, and placed in human hands "to solve the crucial problems and simplify the difficult situations of a people seeking liberty, life, peace and happiness in a land and government of their own."[24]

We must notice his initial incentives to place the Back-to-Africa movement in a biblical context. For he immediately proceeded to contextualize the Moses\Exodus experience with the plight of the Negro in America, and the religious challenge that God had placed before them. He said:

> *"Let me summon, as it were, four such stalwart ones and as each stands before you put to him the question of the text, 'Negro, what is that in thine hand?' The first replies, 'The Rod of Political Destiny.' Negro, what is that in thine hand? The second replies, 'The Rod of Industrial and Commercial Achievement.' Negro, what is that in thine hand? The third replies, 'The Rod of Financial Acquisition.' Negro, what is that in thine hand? And the fourth replies, 'The Rod of Spiritual Freedom.' They are correct. Within their hands they hold the dynamic combination by means of which the aims and hopes and aspirations of this noble Race are to be realized."*[25]

He then proceeded to discuss the implications of each of the 'Rods,' expounding at length on the ideals and objectives of the UNIA, and showing how they had so far made a significant difference to the lives and circumstances of some Blacks in New York. Under the 'Rod' of Financial Acquisition, for example, he observed that Negro businessmen in Harlem had prospered because of the social and ideological stimulus provided by the UNIA. "Such are not men who seek its destruction, for they possess enough business acumen to capitalize its spirit of race consciousness and convert it into an asset."[26] It was, quite understandably, with the 'Rod of Spiritual Freedom' that he waxed most eloquent, calling it the "original rod in the Negro's hand... A slave in body, he nevertheless felt free in soul, since none could deny him the solace of religion. More religious by nature than other races, Negroes neglected their political, industrial and financial progress, content to sing 'It is well, it is well with my soul.'"[27]

McGuire contended that if the Negro was to advance, the Negro needed religion, but at the same time there had to be limits to the control which religious institutions had on the Negro. "The material without the spiritual is as bad as, nay, worse than the spiritual without the material."[28] This required freedom in theology, in ritual and in control of religious organizations for "spiritual freedom is the basis of all other freedoms." Such spiritual freedom consisted of representing God in the color of the Negro's own likeness. Why should Negroes continue to believe that God was white? Further, he said: "Refuse to have your children taught any longer the white man's catechism which requires them to 'submit myself to all my betters, and to order myself lowly and reverently.' Fellow men, if you did not realize it before, realize it now, that only Negro pastors and bishops can be true shepherds of Negroes. Some white ministers pretend and some few try to be, but they just simply cannot."[29]

As McGuire drew his sermon to a close, he commented on the significant contribution of Marcus Garvey to the UNIA, and how important it was that Garvey himself recognized that the UNIA was a spiritual movement. He then issued this final challenge:

> *"Negro, in your hand you have carried the rod for several years, but only to a limited extent has it been of service. Cast it down today at the feet of the Omnipotent, and see! See how the seemingly inanimate and inert thing becomes instantaneously a creature pregnant with life and energy and motion! Cast down before the King Immortal and Invisible this organization to be baptized with the new birth, and joyful wonder and glad surprise you shall witness the glorious and victorious achievements of all its aims and objects."*[30]

With a prayer taken in the main from the Book Of Common Prayer, he commended the UNIA to God's protection and guidance. Afro-Evangelism had taken a popular theme from the Old Testament, and had contextualized it in such a way, and grounded it in the realities of social, economic, and political aspirations for disenfranchised masses, and had given it a new thrust for emancipatory action and spiritual and religious invigoration. Joseph Robert Love had inspired Marcus Garvey; Marcus Garvey had inspired George Alexander McGuire; and McGuire had committed his brilliant eloquence, his religious fervor and theological acumen to further the vision of advancement for the Negroes of his day, particularly in the movement founded by Garvey. Since he could not accomplish these designs within the fold of an institution presumably committed to the Gospel of Jesus Christ, he sought to accomplish them through the agency of a non-ecclesial popular movement, which nevertheless possessed the spiritual fervor and moral commitment of the people of God. For the people of God, outside of the Church of God, still remain the people of God. Garvey was a Roman Catholic, McGuire, as an Afro-Anglican Extract, founded his own church, but neither sought to proclaim that God was captive to their peculiar religious affiliations. McGuire had already discovered the hard way that God was not an Episcopalian either.

As we take our leave of McGuire for now, three brief points must be noted. First, there can be no doubt that McGuire always wanted to be a bishop, and both our documents speak to this personal ambition of his. Second, after his death in 1934, grave leadership problems afflicted the AOC which he founded; his widow and daughter returned to the Episcopal Church. Three, one of the notable admissions into the AOC ministry was the Rev. Reginald Grant Barrow, a Barbadian minister of the AME Church, who had himself been an Afro-Anglican Extract. Barrow's story is also a fascinating one, as he tells it himself, and we would do well to turn next to this further link in the J. Robert Love chain of influence. Love inspired Garvey, Garvey inspired McGuire, McGuire consecrated Barrow as an AOC Bishop on September 8, 1925.

## *Reginald Grant Barrow*

Barrow was another fascinating radical Afro-Anglican prophetic exile at the turn of this century. His early years we will pass by. Suffice it to say that he was a Barbadian trained at Codrington College, my alma mater, made deacon in 1913, and priest in 1914. He served first in the Windward Islands and then returned to Barbados. Among other things, he served as Headmaster of the Alleyne School in the parish of St. Andrew, where my father-in-law, the late Cecil Craig Thompson, was one of his pupils. He left Barbados to work in the Virgin Islands as an Anglican priest late in 1919, where our part of the story begins.

Barrow considered that on leaving Barbados he was leaving behind the bigotry and racism in the Anglican Church, and that he was going to the Virgin Islands, now under the United States' flag, to a new and better world. This was not to be. He assumed pastoral duties at Holy Cross Church, St. Croix, in January, 1920, having acted for a month at a church in St. Thomas. It was that month's sojourn in St. Thomas that was to cause Barrow his Anglican troubles later. He was acting for a white Barbadian priest named Pilgrim, who had actually been a junior to Barrow at Codrington College, and who, on many occasions, had to be tutored by Barrow. Barrow said that Pilgrim was his "Fag" (a title in use at Codrington at the time).

On "Brotherhood Sunday," (the Third Sunday) in January, 1920, Barrow preached a sermon on Christian brotherhood, using the text: *"Lord, we saw one casting out devils and in thy name, and we forbade him. Jesus said, forbid him not."* (Luke 9:49-50). Barrow recounts that he spoke strongly on the need for Christian brotherhood. In his own words: "My own mother was a Catholic; my father was an Anglican. I had a broad outlook on religion. I had no need to be bigoted. So I preached a very strong sermon on the evils of bigotry and narrowness within the church and we sang a hymn saying 'We are not divided, all one body we,' and I emphasized that we should make those words true by the way we live with each other.''[31] Barrow was accused by Pilgrim of preaching an heretical sermon. Pilgrim, he said, was one of those Anglicans ''who thought that God only accepts Anglicans in heaven and that nobody could get to heaven except they passed through the Anglican Communion.'' Barrow had actually attracted many non-Anglicans and non-believers to hear his sermons, to witness his fresh brand of Afro-Evangelism. Pilgrim complained to the Bishop of Puerto Rico and the Virgin Islands, Bishop Collymore who, on his next visit to St. Croix, paid a visit to Barrow at his residence at Enfield Green.

Here the plot quickly thickens. Barrow claimed that the Bishop was obviously shocked to find him living in better circumstances than the Bishop himself, since the Church in Puerto Rico was ''a very poor outfit.'' ''So the first shock to him was to find me, a Black man, living in this palatial home, beautifully furnished ...'' The Bishop informed Barrow of the complaint about his heretical sermon which Pilgrim had lodged with him. Let Barrow tell the story himself:

> *''I was sitting down talking to the Bishop just like a man would talk to another man, because we had finished our other business and we were just conversing; and I had my foot in my lap, you know, crossed like this. So when he told me, I said to him, 'My Lord, Pilgrim is not capable of criticizing nor of understanding my sermons. Well, here was I, a Black man, speaking to a second White Bishop from a cracker state like Tennessee telling him that another White man was incapable of understanding or criticizing my sermons. It was quite a situation. I was quite ignorant of the background of this man at the time. So he said to me, 'I am not accustomed to have my Nigger Clergymen talk to me like that.' That was his answer. So I was so shocked. I said to him, 'My Lord, I have just come from Barbados, and the late Archbishop of Barbados - Bishop William Proctor Swaby, who was a cousin of Queen Victoria, not only an aristocrat, but royalty. I said, 'And when we were together, we cracked jokes and talked to each other just like human beings.' I said I didn't know I was a nigger, or a nigger clergyman. So I got right up and told him I was very sorry that the interview was closed.*[32]

Barrow resigned from the Church immediately and sent his letter of resignation by the coachman to the Bishop that same evening. The next day, Sunday, he explained what had happened to the congregation, who became quite upset. The Bishop's reply to Barrow was simple: ''As far as I am concerned, you may go right now.'' Barrow offered to serve his contracted time of six month's notice of quitting, but the Bishop declined the offer. Thereupon, the congregation attempted to get the Bishop to return to St. Croix to discuss the pastoral ministrations at Holy Cross. They sent telegrams to him in Puerto Rico, gathered to wait for a reply, but none arrived. They had been without a priest for over a year before Barrow arrived. For them, the Bishop's actions were the last straw. Barrow recounted: "Different types of people were all there and they decided that they were going to have nothing more to do with the Episcopal Church. That they had been humbugged too long ... So they said to me, 'Come, let us go,' and they said if you worship under a tree, we will be with you. And we came out of the church and we barred the main church door with a large 2 x 4 Joist, as they called it. They drove long spikes into it, and we left."[33]

The next Sunday, they met under a tamarind tree, for the building which they had secured at Grove Place, one mile away, was too small for the more than 350 persons who had left the church that previous Wednesday. Barrow recalled that the "sensation of this change brought hundreds more on the following Sunday. And they grew and grew as I went on and went on, until by the time I left the place we had over 6,000 - as a matter of fact - the whole Labour Union in the Church. So that we can say we grew from 300 in 1920, to about 6,000 in 1922, when I was expelled from the Island."[34]

What church would all these people belong to now? Barrow did not form his own church as McGuire was about to do in New York; he just led them into another church which welcomed Afro-Anglican extracts. The AME Bishop in Arkansas, William Alfred Fountain, paid a visit to St. Croix shortly afterwards, and formally admitted them into the AME Church. Barrow said, "the presence of the Bishop, the first Black Bishop the people saw in St. Croix, brought a tremendous crowd the day that he received us right under the Tamarind tree, because we could not hold the service anywhere else."[35] So began the history of the African Methodist Episcopal Church in the United States Virgin Islands; it was formed out of the bowels of <u>Ecclesia Anglicana</u>, and weaned by the struggles of Afro-Anglicanism for freedom and dignity.

Why was Barrow expelled from the Virgin Islands? It was because he threw himself fully into the cause of championing the advancement of the colored laborers on the Island of St. Croix, and virtually managed the Labour Union during the prolonged absence of its leader in the United States. The conditions under which plantation workers labored were very oppressive, and the combination of Danish and American law did not proffer any social amelioration for them. To be an advocate for the cause of the laboring classes was therefore considered seditious activity. According to Barrow, "In those days, to be a member of a labour union was more serious than to be a communist today. And the idea of having a labour union was absolutely out of the question."[36] He edited the Union's newspaper, and virtually held sway with the general membership, since most of the members were also members of his new church. It was said of Barrow that "he gave his full support to the labour Union of St. Croix, and helped to demand the poor people's rights from the planters and plantation owners which resulted in higher wages."[37] Controversies arose both within the Union and without; legal cases ensued, and Barrow's adversaries among the planter class prevailed on the Governor to have him expelled. He left in October, 1922, to return to Barbados, but he ended up in the United States after a very exciting saga fit for a Hollywood movie.

Because of his AME connections, Barrow found work in several positions in AME institutions. It was as an Assistant Dean at Edward Waters College in Florida that he met McGuire, who was now looking for men of quality to join in the leadership of his new AOC. McGuire invited Barrow to become a Bishop in his new church in June, 1925. He was consecrated in September as the Bishop of Brooklyn, where he served until 1964. There was, however, one significant sequel to Barrow's involvement in the AOC. In 1927, a major dispute arose in the AOC, and legal battles ensued. The October, 1927 editon of <u>The Negro Churchman</u>, the official organ of the AOC, carried this resolution on its first page:

> *WHEREAS four of our former brethren, to wit, the Right Reverend Reginald Grant Barrow, Rev. George S. Brookes, Rev. John G. Bayne, and Rev. S. O. Perkins, have seceded from our ranks, and organized for themselves a distinct and separate religious body; and,*
>
> *WHEREAS we consider it expedient to indicate our attitude towards these brethren, their followers and their movement:*
>
> *BE IT RESOLVED that we declare their religious body schismatic one with which the African Orthodox Church declines to hold communion, and that its ministers be not permitted to officiate in any manner in our congregations...*[38]

Thus began what was known as the Barrow Schism in the AOC, and such was to continue for many decades. Before his death, however, Barrow was received into the Roman Catholic Church in Barbados, and his orders from the AOC, coming through their source in the American Catholic Church, earned him the rank of Deacon, although he was never formally ordained as such. We must not forget, however, that Barrow was the father of the Prime Minister of Barbados at the time, Errol Barrow, now deceased, and also of the present Governor-General of Barbados, Dame Nita Barrow.

## CONCLUSION

Love, McGuire, and Barrow, in spite of their different stories and backgrounds, had many things in common. They thus provide for us a very graphic picture of the Afro-Anglican search for full human development, by means of religion, during the first quarter of this century. That is still precisely what Afro-Evangelism is all about today. The Good News of the Gospel is that Christ has come that all might have life in all of its fullness. These three early Afro-Anglican prophetic figures wrestled in pursuit of such a vision within the church which they loved, but finding little to encourage or sustain them, they turned elsewhere in varying styles and to differing degrees.

They were products of a British colonial system which was designed to contain them, but which rather propelled them into the wider world of the Americas. Such propulsion enabled them to demonstrate that there was no truth to the myth that the Negro could only make full use of his brawn, but very little use of his brain. They each used the power of their intellect and pens to chart new ways of thinking in newspapers and other media. Their power of eloquence and command of the English language made them each a force to be reckoned with. Love and McGuire added to their skills the power of healing through their medical education. They gave very strong advocacy and commitment to the capacity of the Negro to handle his own affairs, and demonstrated outstanding capacities of leadership with far-reaching results. They took their Blackness seriously; not only as the color of their skin, but also as an existential signification of the God in whom they believed.

In many ways Love, McGuire, and Barrow were men ahead of their time. They were intensely prophetic without actually knowing it. They were active pioneers in ways which they did not fully grasp at the time. They were early champions of a cause for Afro-Evangelism which they did not seek to formulate in any definitive way. They simply proclaimed what they saw to be their response to the call from God to those who shared their ethnic and cultural heritage. For them, justice, freedom, and blackness, were integral contructs of human dignity, and they defied every structure, whether social, religious, or political, which sought to hinder their rights as children of God to struggle to achieve it. The legacy of their challenge to us today lies in the Christian courage to call things by their right names, as we continue to wrestle with the liberating truth of the Gospel of Jesus Christ.

It was not only the Afro-Anglicans from the Caribbean of course who were wrestling with the iniquitous systems of their church. Many Afro-Anglican clergymen in this country (United States) had to strive relentlessly for meaning and effective ministry, for practical ways in which they could justify remaining as ordained leaders of a church which did not accord them much respect, simply because of their color. Separate educational institutions had to be established for the benefit of blacks who could not otherwise expect to receive any higher education. One such institution was St. Paul's College, Lawrenceville, Virginia, established by a prominent Afro-Anglican clergyman, Archdeacon Russell. The following chapter takes the form of sermon delivered at St. Paul's in 1993, and seeks to bring back to our notice the fact that our mission for the advancement of our people of color is far from being accomplished.

## CHAPTER FIVE

## *LEST WE FORGET*
*"CONTROL YOUR MYTHS, WATCH YOUR IMAGES"*

We give thanks for the fruits of many labors, for the tears that have been turned into joy, the doubts that have been overcome by certainty, the feeble knees that have been strengthened to run the race set before them, the pains that have been transformed into redemptive experiences, the prolonged winter of scholastic drudgery that has now given way to the spring of graduation. Yes, we give thanks; and we acknowledge before God that, through no merit of our own, nor any possibility of ever being fully qualified, God has brought us this far by faith. Yes, by faith; not a faith that simply says "I think so;" nor even one that says "I believe;" but rather a faith that says "I believe in order that I may know and understand." It is a faith that goes to work, and never demands a time-out, nor an incomplete grade.

The context of the world in which we live is rapidly changing. It is not the same world it was three or four years ago. It's a different world; not the world of the TV series which bears that name ("A Different World"), but a world of fast changing myths and brutally conflicting images. How does one make one's way through such a world? My answer to such a question is: CONTROL YOUR MYTHS AND WATCH YOUR IMAGES.

The word "myth" has come to mean many things, from a legendary story, to an invented idea, or a fictitious and imaginary thing or person. But a myth is also "an unproved collective belief that is accepted uncritically and is used to justify a social institution" (Webster's Dictionary). This is the sense in which I use it here - a current unproven belief held uncritically by many people. Thus Western prosperity was mainly built on African slavery, and it was supported by the mythic belief that people of African descent were biologically inferior. That myth has never been put to death, and it does not seem to be showing any signs of terminal illness. The word "image" simply refers to a mental representation, that by which we conceive and respond to ideas, concepts, and expectations in life. Images of success are promoted through Sports, the Hollywood ethic, and capitalistic exploitation; images of failure, poverty, and violence are widely colored black and brown; images of accomplishment are situated in suburbia, riddled with debt, and surrounded by high-tech gadgetry; while images of human sobriety and sound wisdom are painted dull, boring and almost repulsive.

We cannot exist without myths and images in our common life; we cannot use our intellects and imaginations without being influenced and guided by them in some way or other. Ours is naturally a world of myths and images; but in spite of their rapid changes and constant shifts, we are nevertheless struck by the fact that the more things change the more they seem to remain the same. The basic question for us is where do these myths come from, and who gives them their sustaining life? Who has the power to define and interpret them? Who enjoys the rich benefits of their control?

To have reached the point of successful graduation from St. Paul's College, with all its rich and noble historical traditions, must surely mean that one has already begun to weigh and wrestle with these issues long before today. For St. Paul's College is no ordinary College, and a St. Paul's graduate is not just another graduate. St. Paul's came into being in order to fight for Negro control over certain myths and images: Human Dignity, Moral Integrity, Afro-Intelligence, Leadership Capacity, "Brain-plus-Brawn" versus "Brawn-without-Brain," Cultural Difference, Social Justice, Political Equality, Economic Equity and Academic Excellence, to name a few.

Let it not be forgotten by young or old, that the American Church Institute for Negroes (ACIN) was established by the Episcopal Church in 1906 to strengthen institutions maintained by the Church for the advancement of the negro population; institutions such as St. Augustine's (NC), St. Paul's, Bishop Payne Divinity School, St. Athanasius School (GA), Vicksburg Industrial School, St. Paul's Industrial School, and St. Mark's School. Bishop Kinsolving, in his sermon to the General Convention at Richmond, in October 1907, warned his contemporaries thus: "The black man of the South, so long neglected, demands your prayerful study. No nation ever faced a graver problem, nor one fraught with more tragic possibilities, than that of the ten million negroes in this land..."

Three years later the Annual Report of the ACIN to the Board of Missions made this observation: "The inability of the Southern States to provide adequate secondary and vocational instruction for Negro youth and the present impossibility of founding and maintaining, where needed, such schools as Hampton and Tuskegee offer a signal and unique opportunity to our church to enter helpfully and vitally into what is perhaps the Nation's greatest and most critical problem, that of equipping the Negro youth for honest and useful life as well as for inspiring and developing manly and womanly character controlled by the spirit of Our Lord Jesus Christ." Institutions like St. Paul's were supported by the Church as a direct response to what was seen as the myth of the Negro problem.

But George Alexander McGuire, an Black priest who worked for a time as Field Officer for the ACIN, and who later founded the African Orthodox Church, sought to confront that myth in his ACIN Report two years later. He wrote:

> *"We do not owe the Negro what we have not, but we do owe the Negro the best that we have. And that the Negro deserves the best we have is, we think, clearly testified by the remarkable fact noted in our current annual report, that of all the Negro college graduates during the last fifty years, of whom there are about 3,000, 53.8 per cent. are teachers and 20 per cent. clergymen. No more striking manifestation of the moral virility and the missionary spirit of educated Negroes than this could be found."*

McGuire was clearly demonstrating to the Church in 1912, that the American myth of the Negro problem was not shared by the Negroes themselves who were given the basic opportunities to better themselves. Moral virility and a missionary spirit were indeed factors of a national solution. They were factors then, and they are still very much factors now.

What are the myths with which we are being constantly challenged today? What are the images that will appeal to modern aspirations and career goals? How do graduates seek to cash in on their newly acquired currency of a diploma? And who honors the credentials they bring? Without question, the myth of Progress and Prosperity will continue to prevail. The myth of Qualification and Competence will follow immediately behind. The traditional cliches of Life, Liberty, and the Pursuit of Happiness will always be in close attendance; as indeed will be the myth of Independence and Self-sufficiency. But how will these myths be brought under control if they are defined and presided over by less than friendly forces and institutions?

This is where the faith of which we spoke earlier comes into play. The faith by which we have come this far is that which we need to be renewed and strengthened for a more purposeful and productive life of selfless service and untiring sacrifice. For let us never forget that however much we can make a living by what we earn, we only make life by what we share. To whom much is given, whether by talent, opportunity or resources, of them shall much more always be required. The five loaves and two fish must somehow come to feed the 5,000 waiting on us to be fed. The courses and programs taught at St. Paul's College instinctively instruct us how make a little go a very long way. The pride and dignity of the St.Paulite tradition will so engender a spirit of loyalty and grateful tribute to the Alma Mater, that social conscience will be sharpened in its alumnae\i, professional excellence will be exemplified, and creative and positive cultural reinforcement will prevail through their efforts.

But can they do it alone? No, they cannot, because the combined evils of

Materialism, Individualism, Racism, Sexism, and Unvarnished Pragmatism will always be in evidence in the myths which seek to control their welfare and livelihood. Where must they turn, if they are to "Control Their Myths and Watch Their Images," rather than allow other people's myths to control them?

In Gospel of John 14:1-14, Jesus reminds us as Christians that He is the Way, the Truth, and the Life, by which we seek and find God. For us who are Christians, Jesus is the Way to God that we know, but we should never be so presumptuous as to suggest that God has no other ways to be found. Our primary challenge is simply to make the most of the Way we know; for to seek and find God always involves the full and fierce confrontation with myths which obscure the face of God, and offer some easier and more attractive alternatives. The Way to God does not consist in escape from the real world, nor does it surrender to compromise and shady deals. The Way to God involves a graduation into the world of harsh realities with its deceptive myths and elusive images, it involves a radical engagement with the forces of evil and injustice, it is committed to the transformation of life for the marginalized and oppressed, and it struggles relentlessly to conquer the verb "to have" by using the verb "to be." The content of character must be eternally more significant in value than the conquest of wealth.

What life-long program does Jesus have to offer us? He offers us the Way. He invites us to control our myths and watch our images by maintaining a <u>vision of human excellence</u>, by sustaining a <u>sense of purpose and direction</u> in knowing where we are going and how to get there, in being seized by a <u>sense of mission</u> for the creation of a better community, especially among those who are less fortunate than ourselves, and by being faithful to our <u>sense of vocation</u> from God to make bad things good and good things better.

He offers us the Truth. He invites us to both a passionate knowledge of the Truth, and also to a diligent acquaintance with the truth of Knowledge. He affirms our belief in the myth that knowledge is power, but he also seeks to convert us to the faith that truth is greater than knowledge, and that it is only in the truth that real freedom can be found. For the God of Truth is not only the fount of all knowledge, but also the source of genuine human freedom. Knowledge that domesticates lacks the Truth that liberates. Jesus as the Truth is surely the Truth that liberates. We are summoned by that God of Truth to transform and liberate others today, tomorrow, and always; for if education is to be the emancipation of the mind, it must also be the activation of the emancipated will. We find our true freedom only as we seek to set others free.

He offers us the Life. He invites us to abundant life; and he challenges us to discover whether or not the myth of the Good Life and the American Dream is to be identified with the realities of God's abundant life. He calls us to "life in all its fullness," and he reminds us that one's life does not consist merely in the abundance of things which one possesses. He invites us to the celebration of Life, celebrating the joy, freedom, hope and disruptive love by which the Service mentality triumphs over the "Serve-us" mentality, Competition loses out to Compassion, Integrity neutralizes Indecency, and Moral stature outlasts Social status.

Vocation, Liberation, and Celebration, these are the triple instruments of cultural, spiritual, moral, and intellectual skill by which we and others can be empowered by God's grace to control the myths of modern life, especially the triple myths of Power, Sex, and Money. These are the tools by which the images of Beauty, Truth and Goodness can be reshaped. These are the virtues that I pray that we will always take with us, planting seeds of freedom, hope and love, and never tiring in our efforts to leave our world a much better place than we found.

CONTROL YOUR MYTHS AND DO NOT ALLOW THEM TO CONTROL YOU. WATCH YOUR IMAGES, AND MAKE THEM WORK FOR YOU AS YOU FOLLOW JESUS AS THE WAY. HOLD PASSIONATELY TO THE TRUTH. CELEBRATE WITH JOY THE LIFE THAT IS AHEAD OF YOU. MAY GOD RICHLY BLESS US ALL. AMEN.

# CHAPTER SIX

# *SHAPE AND SHARE THE VISION*

Who are our campus ministers today? How do they get into such a ministry? Do they just happen to end up there because there is nothing else going? Is the job merely a stepping stone to something more secure in the church? How do campus ministers think of themselves? Who ministers to the campus ministers? Who ministers to their families? How are they trained for the job? What models of ministry do they follow? Who shapes those models? Who evaluates their ministry? What place do campus ministers fill in the totality of the church's ministry? Who listens to them besides the students? Do they simply provide a ministry for the curious, or is it a challenge for the committed? When are they called upon to make serious contributions to the wider life of the church? What difference would it make to the church's ministry if there were no more campus ministers? How long should one remain a campus minister?

These rambling questions are indicative of the complexities involved in any serious attempt to discuss the search for a vision of the future of our campus ministries as a whole. Campus ministers sometimes struggle against feelings of inferiority and irrelevance in the face of intellectual elitism and unvarnished arrogance. They struggle against being made marginal, both in the church and in the academy. Their pangs of loneliness sometimes prevail. Thus, the campus ministry is not merely a ministry in context, it is also a ministry of contest. Let us see what is meant by this distinction.

## *MINISTRY IN CONTEXT*

Sometime ago, I offered elsewhere some basic assumptions about the issue of the meaning of higher education and our involvement in it. I still hold these assumptions to be quite valid. Allow me to summarize them as follows:

    a. *Education is for life, not just for making a living.*
    b. *Education should produce persons with a passion and excitement for serving others.*
    c. *Places of learning should be primarily dedicated towards the shaping of a better society.*
    d. *Places of learning should be held accountable as communities of special gifts, and as laboratories of wholesome human values.*
    e. *The church needs to draw near to such places of higher learning, not only because of the wisdom and knowledge being made available by God to such communities, but also because it needs to draw on such resources to fulfill its own proper mission.*
    f. *The church and the academy are both called to reinforce each other as engines of social emancipation and enlightenment, and social vanguards of human dignity and fulfillment.*
    h. *Campus communities are not the devil's happy hunting-grounds; they are God's rich fields of grace.*

What then is the context of that ministry? How do we attempt to identify concretely the nature and shape of such a multifaceted ministry? How is the mission charted? Some people have said that the campus ministry "is a ministry of presence, confessing the name of Jesus Christ on the campus and providing a place for support, education, fellowship and growth. It is not a ministry of numbers." Such a definition of the campus ministry indicates how some campus ministers have sought to structure their programs, but it still does not provide for us that fundamental understanding of why a presence is required, or what kind of presence we should project. Further, there are some who see the campus minister as providing a counter-presence on campuses, strange, dull, and even ancient. But it is this sense of the counter-presence which can create a deeper impact on the consciousness and ethos of campus life.

Others hold to the view that the campus minister is called "to provide for and nurture the responsible articulation of the life of faith in its plural voice." This articulation and nurturing of the life of faith is critical to any serious approach to campus ministry. There are many other forms of articulation which find their origins on our campuses, and the battle for the minds and innocent lives of bright and promising human beings becomes fierce and subtle, devious and persistent. The counter-presence of which we have just spoken is perhaps the best form of articulation of the faith we confess, for we must never lull ourselves into believing that compromise and accommodation are the thin edge of the wedge of Christian witness. Ours is the call to expound the Gospel of Jesus Christ without apology. Ours is the call to incarnate the meaning of what is demanded of living members in the Realm of God. Ours is the call to announce God's preferential option for the poor and oppressed, to stand for equal justice and mutual respect for all, regardless of their economic status. Such a call as this requires nothing less than the counter-presence of the Gospel itself, for we are always being challenged by that Gospel to row against the tide, to choose the higher alternatives, and to embrace the unexpected as the authentic signs of God's historical design.

Baptists and Episcopalians are not the only ones who are called to such a ministry. The integrity of God's call to campus ministry cannot be grasped apart from its ecumenical dimensions. With ministers and representatives of other persuasions, we are called to affirm a common vocation in the threefold task of proclamation, fellowship and service. We are called to affirm the principles of a shared ministry, to use our individual talents and resources towards a more efficient and effective ministry. We are to demonstrate unequivocally that denominational diversity on any campus is a sign of strength, mutual trust and support, rather than division and competition. It is in the vigorous pursuit of the ecumenical objectives of the Gospel of Jesus Christ that we can more truly achieve that openness and solidarity, without which no genuine experience of liberation can be appropriated.

This ushers in many challenges, and we need to draw attention to at least some of them. There is first of all the challenge posed by a growing attitude of anti-intellectualism in the churches as a whole. We must give full testimony to the fact that our duty to God requires that we love with all of our heart, mind, soul and strength. The search for knowledge, the free and open exchange of ideas, the testing of traditional beliefs and customs, and even the exploration of uncharted ways, are all part of the process of human cooperation with God's creative activity. What seems to be needed more is a greater emphasis on the part of the academic community to search for the integration of the total person, instead of the subtle attempts to create dichotomies between the various human functions, or the waging of battles between head and heart. The search for knowledge is always a search for human wholeness, and attitudes of antipathy to the development of the intellect only serve to stifle that greater level of human enrichment, out of which social maturity and personal integrity generally emerge.

Again, there is the whole question of ethical renewal and social responsibility. While the wider society generally tends to hold to the view that college campuses are likely to be hotbeds of ethical and moral decadence, places where anything goes, laboratories of experimental permissiveness; it seems inherent in the call to campus ministry that we try to bear witness to the very opposite. There can be little doubt that the campuses generally mirror much of what is happening in the wider community, but it is also true that many of our college students are earnestly seeking to correct what they perceive to be wrong in those societies to which they are hoping to return. Campus ministers are constantly challenged to help the academic community to evaluate the ethical and moral fabric of the society it serves, and to offer guidelines and incentives for striving towards higher levels of social witness and human example.

The cultural and racial diversity of our nation as a whole is very strongly reflected on our campuses. This has given rise to an ever-increasing awareness that America is changing rapidly. The myth of a monolithic culture is dead. The reality of a pluralistic society has suddenly dawned upon us; and we are not quite sure how to deal with it. No more can we be driven by patterns of uniformity or conformity. No more can we insist on all persons looking and sounding the same way. The challenges of such a diversity are enormous, and they hold out to the Christian community the obligations of being responsive and responsible. We must struggle against great odds and powerful forces to defend the rights of diverse cultures to appreciate the varieties of gifts with which they have been so richly endowed by God. It is a call to be prophetic. It is a call to be caring and open. It is a call to be fully respectful of the differences which exist between equal partners in our social sharing. It is also a call to learn from each other that "different" does not mean "inferior," and that in many varying ways God makes available special gifts and graces. Those who have eyes to see them, let them see.

These basic affirmations must inform our total sense of vocation to the campus ministry. We are reminded that we are not called to serve within a narrow framework of human endeavor, but that ours is a commission to go into all the world and preach. It is rather frightening for some of us, therefore, when we suddenly realize that all the world has in fact come to us on our campuses. To accept the call from God to minister on campus, radically involves accepting the possibility that we will have to nurture persons, the likes of whom we have never met before, or about whom we had neither heard nor thought. But the fact that they are to be found in the places where we are called to serve must surely suggest that God has somehow sent them to us. The God who creates us in diversity, calls us out of the bondage of our particularity, to serve God's people in the context of their own diversity. Such a plurality of contexts not only poses exciting challenges, it also offers us new insights about ourselves.

For example, because of their differing backgrounds, our students often display varying perceptions of decency, human dignity, personal courtesy, human rights and freedoms, social discipline, and basic expectations. Habits of students often betray varying notions of authority and acceptance. Religious beliefs and human life-styles shape our young ones in different ways, to the extent that when we encounter them we can sometimes feel the force of their upbringing and backgrounds. Further, the pressures of home and family are often compounded by the pressures of their cultural heritage and the new experiences of dealing with their peers.

Plural contexts also involve family expectations of their off-spring. No campus minister should ignore the fact that students are generally an extension and expression of the homes and families from which they come. They virtually bring their families with them, however much they would prefer to claim their own independence, or a sense of newly-found freedom.

Plural contexts are also denoted by economic factors. Apart from the differences in wealth and financial strength which students generally display, there is the deeper issue of the place of economic and material power in the minds and attitudes of our students. Money is indeed a crucial factor in the livelihood and well-being of the normal student, but we must face the fact that it very often separates the "I am's" from the "I have's." Money is obviously a common factor among us, it traverses all cultural barriers, but while there are some who strive to own it, there are those who succumb to being owned by it. This is the context in which we are called to minister on our campuses.

## THE MINISTRY OF CONTEST

Campus ministry is also a ministry of contest. We are constantly engaged in fighting the good fight of faith. It is the combined force of Christ's commission to preach the Gospel to every creature and make disciples, and the constant war being fought on many fronts for the minds and will of God's people, which creates the need for an effective mission and ministry on the campuses of our nation. We dare not ignore either aspect of the mission, nor dare we search for less challenging ways of understanding what God is calling us to become. We are called to be the church in every place, and being the church involves the necessity to fight, not against each other, not among ourselves, not even against flesh and blood. We are called to fight against live forces in our world which manifest themselves in all sorts of configurations, especially amongst our younger and more unsuspecting brothers and sisters. Campus ministry is thus mission and commission. It is both liturgy and litany. It is witness and service. It is a call to fight with all our spiritual might. This is a ministry of contest. There are at least five characteristics which are suggested by such a ministry.

First, there is the **Commission** from Jesus to feed the lambs and the sheep. Second, we have made a solemn **Commitment** to guide our people towards a better vision of themselves and their world, and towards their own sense of commitment to, and responsibility for, a better world for all people. Third, ours is a ministry of **Concern** for the whole personhood of our students which often takes us beyond the trappings and the clappings, right to the heart of what it means to be human. Fourth, it is a ministry of **Communication**, listening to individuals, and learning them quickly; each with their own uniqueness and special qualities, in all their rich and unpredictable diversity. We are to interpret their own world to them, while attempting to speak to the world on their behalf.

The fifth is **Continuity**. The campus ministry has an inherent vocation of its own. It calls for radical continuity and indomitable courage; for only those who endure to the end can either save or be saved. In the midst of all the flux of campus life campus ministers must provide anchorage and stability. In the maze of tremendous diversity and change the campus minister must offer a beacon of light and a sense of purpose.

These five characteristics - COMMISSION, COMMITMENT, CONCERN, COMMUNICATION, CONTINUITY - serve to remind us of what our whole mission is about. They also serve to point us to the way we should approach the challenges of our ministry of contest.

The campus minister must be the champion of that which is radically fresh and honest, that which is openly Christian and hopefully liberative. The campus minister must pursue such a vocation which will enable him\her to embody the struggle for living out the truth of the Gospel. The campus minister must be the professional advocate for those who suffer at the hands of the rich, the powerful and the too-busy-to-care, whether in church, academy or society. The campus minister must continue to be the living\loving friend of outcasts and the oppressed, as students generally think they are. The Church today provides fewer and fewer people who fulfill this task as their divine vocation task. It is a vocation which demands courage, sacrifice, unrelenting compassion, creativity, imagination, patience, modesty, humility and persistence. It causes the loss of friends, but it calls for the love of enemies. It may not bring promotion; but it certainly brings spiritual satisfaction.

Campus ministers are called to be champions of resilience. It is the heart of their job to preach, by word and example, the virtue of holding on to what they genuinely believe about Jesus Christ and the Gospel. They should not be overcome by frustration and diminishing results. They must be living signs of patient endurance, and human symbols of loyal faithfulness, both to their mission and to the meaning of the Gospel. To be a campus minister is to be always functioning on the borders of the wilderness, beyond which some signs of the promised land are already appearing. The campus ministry is thus a vocation in struggle, in contest with other struggles, searching for a vision of a new community. The vision of the new community is inherent in the Gospel of Jesus Christ, and it ushers into our academic world a distinctive missionary sign of the Realm of God. The campus ministry of contest is therefore a mission of missions.

## MISSION OF MISSIONS

We are called into God's mission to share in the broad agenda of shaping a new world, a world that will reflect more faithfully what we mean when we pray for the Kingdom (Realm) of God to come on earth, and to have God's will done on Earth as it is in Heaven. We are called to shape a vision for ourselves and our church that is broader than our church's immediate concerns. Our ministry and witness on our campuses can play a major part in fostering Christian ideals and shaping such a vision. Three factors are requisite here.

First, campus ministers must remain rooted and grounded in the ongoing life of the gathering church in existing congregations. Second, campus minsters must seek to maintain the most fertile possible relationships with ministers other than campus ministers. Third, campus ministers must establish and sustain strong links of communication and fertile bonds of network between fellow campus ministers both near and far. The hindrance to these factors is just plain self-righteous individualism, which can often be fed by the pangs of loneliness to which we have already referred. The cardinal rule is that campus minsters must seek fervently to minister to each other on the basis of vocational sharing and mutual reinforcement for mission. Together they form a very important sector of the army in the battle for the minds and souls of God's faithful people. Campus ministers must never be found behaving like soldiers in retreat, or victims under siege.

Campus ministers must always be ready to listen to others, ready to learn from others, while sharing who we are, and ready to offer leadership of thought and forward movement towards a vision of a common future.

This means that we must minister to the young people as young people, rather than as elements in the maintenance of our traditional programs. Young people across the lines of race and religion share many things in common, and we need to be seen to be in service of these gifts of youth, rather than as exploiters of an immature humanity. Apart from being the hope of the future, our young people are the staff of our present vitality, and the pluralism they provide for us makes life far more exciting than some of the routinized syndrome of guarding the status quo.

Ours is a mission of liberation, and this means that we must make sure that it always remains a Gospel of liberation. That means that it must set us free from any sense of being culturally bound, free from asserting the primacy of any of our cultural accidents in our people's lives, free from the bondage of intellectual or spiritual superiority, and free from the hope that one day all will come to see the light that we have seen all the time. We must always be prepared to travel lightly, be prepared to minister to strangers, and to be ministered to by them. It is good for us to remember that we should not be reluctant to minister to strangers, for, as Scripture says, we are likely to be ministering to angels unawares. This is what makes our ministry on campus truly a mission of missions. We are not called to service the religious curiosity of the campus community, where people merely go to look at what is going on, or at what is being served at the pot-luck supper. We are on a mission of missions where people are invited to commit themselves to go out on fire with the Spirit of Christ's emancipatory presence. Yes, they are looking to go, not simply going to look. Curiosity kills the cat, as they say; but Commitment saves the world. So let us look, at what such an emphasis might entail in our vision for the future.

## LOOKING TO GO VERSUS GOING TO LOOK

The very rationale for a campus ministry is based on the strong sense of obedience to a call to mission from God. Perhaps it would be true to say that nowhere else does the notion of mission come closer to the reality of ministry than in the campus ministry. It is truly a vital mission of God, vital enough to be contagious, vital enough to command not only the constancy of support from the wider church but also the active participation of the non-campus community. This sense of mission must never be lost, principally because of the nature of the God whose mission it is. The God who calls is the God who sends. The God who sends is the God who empowers. The God who empowers is the God who sustains. The God who sustains is the God who comes. The God who comes is the God who calls, and who sends us out again. This is the cycle of the divine mission which wastes no time with the idle or the curious, but generates a constant sense of urgency for the faithful and the committed. Commitment means endurance. Endurance means salvation. Salvation is the only vision of the world's future which makes lasting sense, both on our campuses and in the wider society.

We therefore need to establish some specific target areas for campus mission and ministry. They should include the following:

> a. *The multi-faith environment, where we explore the meaning and vitality of different faiths, or of no faith, without being threatened by these differences.*
> b. *The development of programs of education for wholesome relationships in marriage, or in mature adulthood among singles.*
> c. *The development of new forms of Christian spirituality which would enhance the witness of the Gospel in the face of the contemporary secular and individualistic forces at work.*
> d. *The promotion of a community of witness against racism, sexism, ethnocentrism, hetero-sexism, agism, homophobia, and atheism, and insensitivity to the disabled, as inherent dimensions of the Christian presence.*
> e. *The active support of programs in which students help students to find their true identity and make the fertile adjustments to college life - students must be trained and encouraged to minister to each other willingly and responsibly.*
> f. *We should establish modest programs of dialogue and awareness-building towards the new habits of living in a world based on Peace, and no longer at War, where plowshares replace swords and shovels replace bullets, with all its norms, values, priorities, structures of relationships, as well as its expectations for a richer celebration of our humanity.*

Can these target areas be addressed without some formative vision of the future of the campus ministry? Can we take the risk of pouring new wine into old wineskins? Can we dare presume that these areas will bring new life to our campus ministries under the heading of "business as usual"? If not, what should be the shape of this new vision? Let me conclude by suggesting five constructs of this new vision for the future which I consider to be inescapable for the program agenda I have just outlined.

First there must be a fresh assault of faith on the debilitating forces of our age. I want to call this NEO-FUNDAMENTALISM. This is radicalistic faith that will take up again the root meanings and proclamations of the Gospel without shame or fear, without compromise or manipulation, but without loss of intelligence or escape from contemporary knowledge. Neo-Fundamentalists will take the whole Christian Tradition seriously without being Traditionalists themselves. They will seek to counteract both the so-called Religious Right or Religious Left by being rooted and grounded in that which was once delivered to the saints. They will witness against the state of affairs which Stephen Carter has outlined in his latest book The Culture of Disbelief: "In our sensible zeal to keep religion from dominating our politics, we have created a political and legal culture that presses the religiously faithful to be other than themselves, to act publicly, and sometimes privately as well, as though their faith does not matter to them." (1993:3)

Second, there will need to be a spirit of NEO-MARTYRDOM. Let no one forget that there would have been no Christian Church today if there had been no Christian martyrs yesterday; the seed of the Church is indeed the blood of the martyrs. The great movements of our times have been characterized by strong and courageous martyrs, whether they have actually given their lives or not. A martyr is a full-blooded witness, not a cold-blooded victim. Campus ministries will not survive on lukewarm, half-hearted, fifty-fifty, seasonal witnessing. The courage and fire with which we march for what we demand must be redoubled in our daily march for what we profess. To quote Carter again: "One reason that education is so bitter a battleground in the struggle over the role of religion in American society is that knowledge is seen as the key to power. The preliminary question, however, is what constitutes the key to knowledge." (1993:213) Neo-Martyrdom carries the answer to that preliminary question.

Third, let there also be a renewal of genuine servant-hood. Let us call it NEO-DIAKONIA. To be followers of the Son of Man, who came not to be served but to serve, is never an easy task; especially among those who have been served for most of their young lives so far. But I believe that this can become the most exciting and cataclysmic challenge for campus ministers - by creating increasing numbers of committed servants of the poor, the powerless, the marginalized and the dispossessed, not merely for the duration of the college course, but long into their professional lives as well. They merely have to keep their alumnae(i) busy and committed to what they have once started.

Fourth, we need to rediscover some of the finer graces of what it means to be truly human - good manners, elementary courtesies, social refinement, values of affirmation, and canons of mutual respect. Many of our campus residents enter our colleges without them, there was no one around to impart such things to them. They should not leave college without them. They will not find them in the workplace, or in the public square. Campus ministries will make one of their finest marks by inculcating habits of CHRISTIAN MUTUALITY. *Good Christians display good manners.* There must be no negotiation about that. The world of politics which envelops us all often overwhelms the little humanity we possess. Listen to Carter again: "Religions are moral forces in the lives of their adherents, which means inevitably, that they are moral forces in the political world. And, as with all institutions, a degree of cross-pollination between religion and politics is inevitable. But when secular political considerations become prior to, rather than subsequent to, religious considerations, the result is not cross-pollination but pollution." (1993:81)

Finally, campus ministers may be our last hope for the REJUVENATION OF THE CHURCH. The Church which was founded by a band of young people, and whose pioneer died at a very early age, is now been completely dominated, controlled and defined by those who can no longer claim to be such. Qualification for entry into the Kingdom was described as being similar to being young, but we have overturned such a criterion by insisting that the young must imitate the old. The future of campus ministry is inextricably bound up with the future of the church, and I do not see how either will have a future unless we are rescued by the younger generations; however much we kick and scream about holding on to power and traditions of our authority. Let campus ministries become more subversive of the growing gerontocracy in the church. Let them infiltrate all the pews, altars, pulpits and vestry-rooms with younger blood, fresh commitment, unspoilt religious habits and new visions of God's beautiful world.

Two Episcopalian writers, Richard Kew and Roger White admitted the following: "A further example of our shortsightedness has been the de-emphasizing of campus ministry, the threshold over which the church's future leadership has so often passed." (1992:5) But then later in their book, New Millennium New Church, they have this to say: "America's is an aging society, and ministry to and by the elderly could become a major point of possible growth and contention as the 1990's proceed. It is inevitable that, as the baby boomers enter the final portion of their active business lives, we will be forced to rethink many facets of our culture in light of this overload of senior citizens." (1992:168) Whatever you choose to make of the godly gentlemen's assertions, let us not forget that the baby boomers' babies are already with us, and that they are our best hope for the rejuvenation of the church from the very top to the bottom. We need the young people to come over and help us to be the church again. Campus ministers hold a good part of the key to the future.

In conclusion, let us remember that the days on our college campuses are always days of great exploration, experiment and expression. They are days of discovery, discernment and decision. They are days of curiosity, of going to look at whatever is around, tasting it, trying it out, hanging around. The future of America passes through our hands, our ministries, our pastoral and preaching moments; yes, even through our spiritual and moral leadership. Let us resolve to accept that spirit of curiosity as an opportunity sent to us by God, and let us seek to transform it into a passionate commitment for Christ and the Gospel through the five factors which I have just outlined. They may have just gone to look, but let us create in them a new spirit so that they might look to go out for Christ. For when curiosity becomes commitment, ministry has already created a new mission, and the vision of the new creation is already becoming reality. In days like these when the forces of evil are so strong, we have no time to waste. Let us not think ourselves into the vision of the future; let us act out the future in our opportunities of today.

## CHAPTER SEVEN

# CHRISTIAN PARTNERSHIP FOR SOCIAL CHANGE

"Things got so bad with me that I went to my half-brother, with whom I had never been close, to ask him for help. He is an Anglican priest, a widower living in New Jersey in a three-bedroom house. I hoped he could help me in some way until I could pull myself together.
'If I don't get some help, I'm going to wind up living in a shelter,' I told him.
'Who runs the shelter?'
'Carmelite nuns.'
He gave me a cup of tepid coffee and sent me on my way to my first experience in shelter living. I have lived in six different shelters here in the District. It's an awful life. No one would choose it."[1]

So ran the testimony of a homeless woman some years ago, aged 53. She had been born in Brooklyn, New York, the holder of a master's degree in teaching from Columbia University, and a daily worshipper at one of Washington's prestigious churches. "My home is a lonely bed in a dreary D.C. shelter," she said. The plight of the so-called street people (or bag-people), have to do with the church's understanding of itself, and of its role in society.

### POVERTY: SIGN, SYMBOL, AND SIN

Perhaps the spectacle of the thousands of America's sons and daughters sleeping on the park-benches, and grates, and in the doorways of city buildings, all across the country, has become so common-place that it no longer raises questions about common notions of duty, or dignity, or even decency. If there is no perceptible connection between those who are comfortably snuggled in bed and those who are confined to the wilds of urban cold and nakedness, then the fact of society has faltered, the faith of society has faded, and the friction in society has festered. For the Christian, however, homelessness represents so much of a symbol, a sign and a sin, that the spectacle cannot be ignored.

As symbol, homeless people remind us of the father of our faith, Abraham, the wandering Aramean. They remind us of the Son of Man who claimed that unlike the foxes and the birds he too was homeless, with nowhere to "lay his head" (Luke 9:58). They remind us of the nature of our stay on earth, that we have here no permanent abode, no "abiding city." They remind us of the provisional dimension of God's church, that it is a pilgrim community on the way with Christ. They remind us of ourselves, that there, but for the grace of God, we too would find ourselves. We could go on and on drawing out the range of symbolism which the plight of the homeless provides. But alas, homelessness is more than symbol, it is fact; and we would need to consider very seriously the ethical implications of converting facts into symbols merely for our spiritual illumination.

As sign, the fact of homelessness points us to the mores by which we live in the "land of the free and the home of the brave" - the homeless are free to sleep on the streets and brave to contend with the elements of nature. Yet there is a further point beyond such 'freedom' and 'bravery'; it lies in our own courage to be complacent and accommodating with such manifestations of human volition, or indeed, the lack of it. As sign, homelessness points us to the reality of the human condition in the world at large; for if the homeless fare like this in the richest country in human history, how much worse off must be the plight of others in poorer lands? There are those who say that America's homeless are a sign of a stark indisposition of a strangely disposable society. Homelessness may often be the result of one's own indiscretions, or it may result from mental illness, or from plain economic disaster. Whatever the cause, it still constitutes a sign that something is wrong with the way in which we respond to social reality, especially as it is experienced by those on the underside.

Poverty and loneliness are national and global problems, but we tend to classify them as problems for the individual and not for the society, welfare payments and unemployment benefits notwithstanding. A society that increasingly fails to protect its unprotected demonstrates unwittingly a structural poverty in itself that is not diminished by pretensions of wealth, power, or status. There is a poverty of the human spirit to which the plight of homelessness radically points, one which we share in common, and which also challenges our claims to social maturity, or to increasing levels of enlightenment and accomplishment.

As sin, we can readily recognize the fact of estrangement and alienation endemic in the social order, when our people once loved are now consigned to levels of existence more wretched than we would ever wish for ourselves. We can sense the nature of human punishment, whether self-inflicted or socially permitted, when some of our nations' once promising sons and daughters resign themselves to lives of patent degradation. We can feel the guilt so painfully exposed when some of our own kith and kin prefer to rediscover some sense of belonging with others who like themselves have come to regard themselves as outcasts. We can detect the blatant abuse of human free-will, when some of America's most favored resources - humanity - are allowed, or implicitly encouraged, to choose a life of inhuman solace and unwholesome refuge. Estrangement, alienation, punishment, guilt, abuse of free-will, are all part of the grammar of sin, as Christians understand it, and the major source of social friction is brought into play when the structures of sin are made to re-inforce the foundations of social well-being. Someone pays the price, and it is usually the poor and the homeless down-trodden.

The church is expected to see itself as the poor often see themselves - they stand in need of God, and they are the guaranteed inheritors of the Kingdom of God. New Testament christologies are incomplete without some basic reference to the Christ who becomes poor, and who is then exalted by God. Poverty may have many dimensions, but it certainly allows for no ambiguities. Poverty is poverty, and the poor are really poor. Gestures of symbolic poverty, however well-intended, often assault the dignity of the poor, who, after all, retain their status as beings made in the image and likeness of God. Further, efforts to fight poverty sometimes result in fighting against the poor themselves. The poor are those who lack the prospects of gaining reasonable access to the basic needs of wholesome livelihood. There will always be such classes in the world, for one reason or another. They nevertheless represent the focus of the church's evangelical task - to preach the good news to the poor, to provide both the bread _of_ life, and the bread _for_ life.

There is therefore no need for us to look again at what it means to be poor. The problems of poor people are very well known, but for many of us, they are known from the outside. I was brought up on a number of proverbial sayings from my elders, through which I learned much of the local folk-wisdom. One of the sayings I learned as a child was that "only they who feel it, know it." Regardless of how much we attempt to analyze poverty from the outside, it is never the same thing as those who are actually poor. It is very important for us to recognize and acknowledge that the poor are really poor.

## PEOPLE RICH - PEOPLE POOR

Now if there are the poor of the world, then there are also the rich people. It is this great divide between people who are really rich and people who are really poor which continues to give us cause for concern. Just because we are Christians, the awful scandal of the divide between rich people and poor people is a serious challenge to the nature of our Christian belief and practice, as well as to the shape of our Christian conscience, or the depth of our Christian responsibility.

It has been generally claimed that when people are really rich, they experience many problems. One of the problems they are said to encounter is, why should they share their wealth with others? For many of them, the whole point about getting seems to be that it is not the basis for sharing, but simply the basis for getting more.

Jack Nelson, in his book, <u>Hunger for Justice</u>, (Orbis, New York), suggests at least five reasons why it is so difficult for the rich to share their wealth. His suggestions are worth repeating here.

First, Nelson says that wealth has a mesmerizing effect on the rich. It mesmerizes the rich because, for the most part, they are isolated from the conditions of the poor and the marginalized. They just do not know how the other half, the other part, of the world lives. So the rich, most of the time, exist in blissful ignorance of those on the other end of the social and economic spectrum.

Second, Nelson suggests that when one is rich, it is difficult to hear God's word being addressed to one as judgement. Why? Because wealth is rather to be regarded as a sign of God's favorable disposition to the wealthy. After all, is there not the promise of milk and honey? Is there not a biblical precedent suggesting that when things are going well, it is a sign of divine favor? Thus any word from God that suggests that there is judgement or displeasure, (*"Woe to you who are rich..."* James 5:1), is difficult to accept.

A third reason given by Nelson is that, for rich people, wealth becomes an arrogant symbol of the viability of their political economy, as well as the validity of their religious cult. In other words, not only are they all right and doing the "right thing," but they also have the tangible results to show for it. So there is something very comforting, something very reassuring, that, if things are working well there must be something good in what we are doing. Success is supposed to speak for itself.

Fourth, Nelson says that God's word is difficult for the rich, because it demands justice. Justice as sharing, justice as participation in the lives and painful plight of the people on the underside just does not make much sense, at least it is not a very attractive proposition for the wealthy.

The fifth reason suggested by Nelson is that rich people always tend to be on the defensive about their wealth, for they feel that they are only attacked by others simply because they are rich, and that those who criticize them are jealous of their wealth. Thus they guard themselves very carefully against people who come close to them, because they are conscious of the fact that those who draw near are often being attracted only by their wealth.

So these five reasons, Nelson suggests, are very significant in the lives of rich people; and they create problems for them in any attempt that they might make to share their wealth with others, or be concerned for their welfare.

In November 1987, the Roman Catholic Church published an Encyclical Letter to mark the 20th anniversary of "Populorum Progressio." It was entitled <u>On Social Concerns</u>. In it, Pope John Paul II paid much deference to the high ideals espoused in

Populorum Progressio and to his predecessor, Pope Paul VI. He reiterated and reaffirmed many of the concepts and styles of theology that were therein enunciated, and dealt with some issues of development concerning the poor.

There are a few points in that Encyclical to which I would draw some attention for purposes of our present discussion. The first is that it sought to make development a concern for everyone, and that was an important advance. Development is not just a concern for the poor and the underprivileged in the Third World. Development is a global concern for everyone, because development is at work everywhere.

A second point is that for the first time the Vatican was giving added currency to the notion of the Fourth World. This was a significant contribution to the context of developmental concerns. For a period of time during the oil and food crises of the early 1970's, there was frequent talk of six "worlds," based on their economic conditions existing at the time. Those which were most seriously affected by the crises were at the bottom of the ladder; those developing countries which had oil were in a higher order than those which did not. In other words, the Third World was subdivided into four categories. But since that period, we seem to have settled for four categories overall, a First, Second, and Third World, as well as a Fourth World. It is interesting to note that the notion of a Fourth World had to do with pockets of poverty and deprivation in the rich countries. So the Fourth World was even to be found in Washington, D.C. The homelessness that exists is one of the indicators. The widespread unemployment is another. Third, there is the whole problem of international debt on the part of the richest countries in the world. These are indicators of the existence of the Fourth World.

A third point in the Encyclical was the notion of Underdevelopment being contrasted with Superdevelopment. Here the Encyclical suggested that Superdevelopment was a term that should represent such things as undue consumerism, waste, and the ecological decay that have taken place in industrialized countries. Here however, I would take issue with the word "superdevelopment" and would prefer the use of the word "mal-development." It is not "super" at all. "Super" means above. "Super" means beyond. "Super" suggests something in an advanced state. But that is not what was meant. So it is "mal-development" because the values of human intercourse and human relationships, the values of getting and spending, the values of social priorities that should contribute to the common good were in serious disarray. We cannot claim to be far long the road to development when the basic elements of human livelihood are seriously under siege. My suggestion to the Vatican would have been to drop "Superdevelopment" and to think of "Mal-development" instead, for that was really what we were concerned about.

Fourth, the Encyclical paid particular attention to sin in its structural dimension. Sin, for the Roman Catholics at least, was not just being discussed at the individual and personal level, requiring the regularity of a visit to the confessional, as in popular Catholic piety. It was being recognized that there were structures of sin which militated against the processes of development, and that unless and until these were acknowledged and properly named, then the means of liberation from the grasp of such demonic structures would not be realized.

I found one quotation in the Encyclical to be quite interesting:

> *"Development which is merely economic is incapable of setting man free. On the contrary, it will end by enslaving him further. Development that does not include the cultural, transcendent and religious dimensions of man and society to the extent that it does not recognize the existence of such dimensions and does not endeavor to direct its goals and priorities towards the same, is even less conducive to authentic liberation. Human beings are totally free only when they are completely themselves in the fullness of their rights and duties. The same can be said about society as a whole. The principal obstacle to be overcome on the way to authentic liberation is sin and the structures produced by sin as it multiplies and spreads. The freedom with which Christ has set us free (Galatians 5:1) encourages us to become the servants of all. Thus the process of development and liberation takes concrete shape in the exercise of solidarity. That is to say, in the love and service of neighbor especially the poorest,"*

I found that last to be a most powerful phrase. We must notice the association of four very important dimensions. There is service and development. There is liberation and solidarity. These are four key words which all go together. So much for the Papal Encyclical. It represented an important statement in the universal concern for Christian participation in the struggle against poverty.

## MISSION AND DEVELOPMENT

For the most part, we should never be found separating notions of development from a sense of vocation for mission. Mission and development are inseparable. As we discussed in Chapter Three, mission is central to Christian theology, because mission derives its meaning from the character of God. Mission is actually an aspect of the doctrine of God, rather than an aspect of the doctrine of the church. Very often, this is where so much of our preference for what makes development Christian begins to be obscured. We tend to believe that mission has to be defined in terms of an objective reality, and that it is primarily concerned with conversion, or individual salvation, or church extension, or even proselytism. Mission should not be understood in terms of having to withstand, or to confront, the processes of secularization.

We should never lose sight of the fact that mission is evangelism plus social action. Why? Because it represents the totality of the task which God has set for the church. It is the God who is known primarily in the changes of the world who sends the church on a mission of constant movement and change in a changing world. A church in mission is a church that is living for others, a church that is not concerned with itself. Indeed I would say that a church that is on mission from God is a church that is turned inside out, entirely and always turned towards the total emancipation of the world as a whole.

So mission means proclamation, yes. But it also means witness and service. They go together. If this is so, then mission is not primarily our activity as missionaries, or as participants in social praxis. But mission is essentially God's activity, and the church is constantly involved in seeking and struggling for renewal, for reconciliation in the world, because God in Christ has reconciled us. God takes the whole world very seriously, and it is because we believe in this world-affirming God that we must also come to understand what it means to believe in a sending God who, in that act of divine affirmation, sends us, the church, into that world. For us as Christians, therefore, there can be no disjuncture between salvation history on the one hand, and world history on the other. The history of the world is at one and the same time the history of God affirming and saving the world.

Ion Bria's affirmation that "mission is understood as an actualization of God's economy of salvation" is also very important here. If we are to be concerned with understanding the nature of mission as an integral dimension of our understanding of the nature of God, then a number of factors from the Gospel tradition begin to strike us with fresh vigor.

Compassion takes on some very important dimensions. The sense of duty emerges. This sense of duty is always before us, but we must never forget that for the Christian it emerges first from the Gospel. There is also the sense of debt; we owe it to others to be actively concerned with, and responsive to, their needs. Or again, there is the sense of obedience. What is the nature of divine authority in our lives, as we seek to live it out in Christian witness? Compassion is a debt that we owe to God's people in loving obedience to God's law of compassion.

There is also the concept of stewardship. If stewardship means only acquiring the gifts of God and then determining how they are to be used for our good, then that is limited. But if stewardship means our trusteeship of God's gifts for God's works, then another dimension begins to appear.

At the center of our liturgical life is the primacy of sacrifice. For the whole church, the Eucharist becomes central. The whole point about the Eucharistic act is that it is the re-presentation of the once-for-all sacrifice of Christ. It is the liturgy of sacrifice, which takes place at the altar; then there is an altar spread abroad in the world where that sacrifice has to be implemented also. It is the sacrifice in the world linked with the sacrifice in the church, in the liturgy, that makes a very important statement about what we understand to be the demands of the Gospel.

Another word is mutuality, the sense of becoming who we are together, and out of the central meaning of the Gospel. It is made clear to us that we are always on the way to becoming who we are already. The theology of the early church, especially that which we meet in the Johannine literature, holds up to us the fact the we are already children of God, but we are not sure who we are to become. But in the meantime, we are to help one another in this process of becoming who we are.

If development is going to make sense for the Christian, then it has to take its root in the heart of the Gospel, and these Christian ideals and virtues, which that I have just briefly enunciated, must in some way be the hallmark of the enterprise.

## UNDERSTANDING DEVELOPMENT FOR THE CHRISTIAN

What are we talking about when we speak of "Development"? Most people have their own working definition of development. The development experts have their favorite definitional approaches. Yet we are always in search of new definitions. I think it is true to say that development is always a developing concept. We need to recognize this when we seek to review the classical goals of development. Seven goals appear to me to have been constant ever since development became a popular word over forty years ago.

The goals were as follows:

1. *The generation of self-awareness about the human condition.*
2. *The creation of catalysts for economic growth.*
3. *The promotion of a spirit of self-reliance by enlarging people's capacity to generate and sustain indigenous development efforts.*
4. *The promotion of wider participation of people in the social and political process.*
5. *The generation of new ways of reconciling estranged groups in society.*
6. *The creation of a just, participatory and sustainable society.*
7. *The identification of more efforts towards the realization of full humanity.*

The developmental theories, approaches, and strategies which have been propounded over the years, have tended largely to be variations on these themes; the seven goals for development have remained pretty much in place.

How then does the Christian attempt to pursue these goals? What is that call from the Christian faith that beckons us individually and collectively to deal with a response to these goals? From a theological point of view, we should recognize that the way we try to interpret and live out our faith in the world has some important implications for the working out the elements of that faith in development practice itself. Let us explore a few examples.

Take our Christian doctrine of the world--the world in which we live. Whose world is it? Christians say it is God world. But yet, is it not true to say that Christians very often prefer to become engaged in a battle between their profession of theistic faith and their pursuit of deistic practice? By that I mean, although we profess that God is intimately and intricately involved in the affairs of the world, so much of our activity and our policies say to God, "Leave us alone, we're getting on with the business of running the world as we like. Don't interfere with it. We will operate it for you. Don't interfere with the structures which we have set up. Don't talk to us about justice and redistribution because that will spoil everything. You have set certain things in place, do not rearrange them."

It is quite unfortunate that some of the attempts we make to blur the edges that normally divide us socially and economically would seem to some Christians to be an affront to God's divine will and purpose.

We need to remember therefore that in our concern for believing in the world as God's creation, that it is not true that God has ordered our estate, and it is not true that accidents of our birth and circumstances are a direct reflection of God's divine will. What is true is that wherever we are, whatever our circumstances are, we are expected, and called by God, to participate in some kind of divine creative activity which is still ongoing. Unless and until we think of creation, not in static terms but in dynamic ongoing terms, and stop talking about creation, and start talking about divine creativity, and acknowledge that God's creative work is going on, several factors will continue to be robbed of their meaning. "Oikoumene" does not remain indicative of a fixed state of affairs, the status quo. God's "oikoumene" becomes a movement, a movement for change; and, in that process, wherever there is "oikoumene," then there is "oikonomos," the economy. We are involved in God's economy, working with God in bringing about some kind of creative activity on behalf of God.

Let us look at a second example. How about our understanding of who we are as individuals, as persons, as human beings? Let us call it Christian anthropology, the doctrine of being human. Christians have always held to an understanding of the belief that human life is sacred. Human life is sacred. What causes problems in the Christian world is the extent to which that principle is variously promulgated. But there can be no denial of the basic fact that Christians believe that human life is sacred and therefore has to be ministered to. At the very least, among the residues that come to us out of the Jewish tradition, mainly from the Hebrew Scriptures, is the belief that we are beings made in the image and likeness of God.

At the very center of our faith, we have an incarnational foundation for our religion. Christianity is incarnational. It is something which always has to be fleshed out, for our faith stands on the affirmation that the Logos (Word), which was God, became flesh. It did not become concept; did not become stone; but the Logos became flesh - flesh and blood. So that the body - your body or mine - is central. It is pivotal to our whole understanding of what it means to be Christian, and therefore to what it means to pursue a religion of salvation towards wholeness. Therefore, all anthropology, all Christian anthropology in practice, demands that we put in place lines of approach, and strategies, that will take the human body seriously. Wherever the human body is in jeopardy -- malnutrition, hunger, bondage, unjust incarceration, drought, famine, race -- whatever it is, wherever the human body is in trouble, there the incarnational response of religion is beckoned by the God who has made all people in the divine image.

Or again, let us take the central aspect of our faith - the doctrine of Christ, Christology. Jesus Christ is for us, I think, a historical and mystical sign of sacrificial giving. We practice Christology in our liturgy. We practice Christology in the proclamation of the Word. What is difficult however is to practice Christology in the world at large. How do we put our understanding of the doctrine of Jesus Christ to work in God's world? It is always very difficult. We can talk about it; we can update our books, we can publish new position papers - but putting it to work becomes difficult. Is there such a thing as a practical Christology? I believe that there is. Jesus Christ made his manifesto very clear. He said, *"I have come that people might have life and that they might have it in all of its fullness."* (John 10:10)

Thus the nature of the Christic mission, the nature of the mission of Christ, was towards the full humanity of all persons. What does the search for full humanity mean? It takes us into all kinds of policy decisions. It takes us into a radical re-evaluation of how we perform our liturgies, yes, but also how we put into practice the understanding of those liturgies in the world. I therefore hold to the view that a Christology devoid of its sociological and missiological implications in the world is hardly valid. Christ still has to be identified in "the least of these," whom he calls his brothers and sisters.

Let us take a final example. Let us look at the question of the Kingdom of God. We pray in the Lord's Prayer: *"Thy Kingdom come. Thy will be done on earth as it is in heaven."* We are praying for the coming of that Kingdom of God into our own historical condition. Quite rightly the Encyclical suggested that no secular, or historical, or human organization on earth could be equated with our understanding of the Kingdom of God. At the very least, we can speak of the church as a sign of that kingdom, for the kingdom is yet to come. It is always on the way. What does this mean? It means that if the Kingdom of God is on the way, we who are the church as a sign of that kingdom enjoy a provisional form of existence. Nothing is set. Nothing is fixed. There is no such thing as the status quo that remains in place. The structures of the kingdom are light, fluid, and flexible, and they move not only with fresh outpourings of the Holy Spirit, but also with fresh outpourings of insights from God Who is bringing that kingdom in little by little.

At the very least, the prayer for the Kingdom of God to come among us is at one and the same time a prayer that we will see ourselves as being involved in a movement that runs aslant across every structure in the world. It is not a prayer for God to baptize and sanctify the systems which we put in place. It is a prayer for God to bring them under the judgement of the kingdom. It is a prayer for God to turn them inside out again, because as soon as we become too comfortable with them, something goes wrong. The constant dying and rising, the constant going and selling all, and giving, and getting more to give yet again, is what it is all about. "Thy Kingdom come" then means a constant recognition that this pilgrim community called church is moving forward in the light of a new age that is not yet, but which is assured, because the Christ, who is also the Kingdom has already made it possible through his ministry, his death, and his resurrection.

The other side of that Kingdom of God is that we need to live lives not only that are flexible and provisional, but lives that are anticipatory of something more, something greater. We must live as if we understand what that kingdom is. We must live in terms of our relationships, in terms of the getting and disposal of resources, in terms of our structures. We must live as if we are playing heaven. What do I mean by playing heaven? When I was a little boy, we used to play "Mama and Papa." Someone cooked the food. Someone washed the clothes. Someone went out to work and brought back the wages. We were looking forward to the day when, in 20 years' time, we would be married and have our own house, and so forth. We did that as children, anticipating the future. We anticipated the future.

Something of this kind of anticipatory play is expected of the Christian. We anticipate the fullness of God's Kingdom in our circumstances now. There can be no notion of the Kingdom of God without the practice of justice. There can be no notion of the Kingdom of God without a radical determination to share the resources of the world equitably. There can be no clear understanding of the Kingdom of God with these wide disparities between rich and poor remaining in place. So if development is to be Christian, it has to be Christian at the very point where Christians are involved in bringing into their own life circumstances what they understand the realization of the Kingdom of God to mean. They know it is not yet, but at least they are anticipating it, because there is abundant warning that they cannot come close to the altar, they cannot approach the throne of grace, they cannot even begin to think of drawing near to God, while leaving their fallen and broken brothers and sisters behind. We must all come together, strong and weak need each other.

## DEVELOPMENT IN THE BIBLE

In addition to these theological implications about the developmental imperative which we have just been discussing, and which seem to me to be of utmost importance in our understanding of development for the Christian, we would do well to briefly explore some of the biblical foundations for our developmental concerns. We might best do so by using the optic of the seven goals of development we discussed earlier.

First, in the Bible we find that the equivalent of development must mean having the will to change things. If we use a rule-of-thumb definition for development, we could simply say that development is change, <u>change for the better</u>. The biblical tradition is replete with the constant call for a will to change things. "Metanoia" is a New Testament word. It means repentance; or thinking again; it is a radical right about turn. So that will to change things is here. Development has to with conversion and repentance; and repentance is a precondition for entry into the Kingdom of God.

Second, we might see development suggested in the Bible as responsible change. It is not change for the sake of change, not change in the willy-nilly, but a freedom that has social implications and social responsibility attached to it. We are to change things with an atmosphere of maturity and responsibility. Why? Because we are stewards.

Third, we might see development as having a principal concern for the poor and the powerless. Somehow or another, God always takes an unconditional stand on behalf of the poor and the oppressed. If that is so, then power is that which has to be shared, and power is that which has to transform the circumstances of those who are on the underside of the structures of power. At the very least, power is involved in meting out justice to those who are the victims of injustice. It is about protecting the unprotected. Psalm 72 is perhaps a good example of the duty of the anointed of God. The Lucan Jesus identifies himself with the mission of Isaiah 61 towards setting prisoners free, giving sight to the blind, binding up the broken, bringing good news to the poor.

Fourth, we might see in the demand for justice itself, God's "dikaiosune," God's righteousness, emerging. We have in so many different ways the obligation to work out in our social relationships, and in the building of our social structures, what it means to believe in a just God. Loyalty to a righteous God always carries with it the inescapable obligation of reflecting that divine character in the ethical duties and priorities of Christian behavior.

A fifth aspect would be the search for full human development. This is particularly relevant in the New Testament witness. How else can we read the Beatitudes in Matthew or Luke? How else can we understand what Jesus is doing in the first eight chapters of Mark's Gospel, where Mark chooses his miracle stories and the little sermon excerpts of Jesus very carefully, and they all focus on those on those who are on the underside, even the demoniacs, and those who are hungering for food. There is a search for the fullness of life which seems to emanate from the Bible.

A final aspect might be the building of community. Here we are in the midst of what we might call a practical pneumatology, a study of the doctrine of the Holy Spirit. Not only is the Holy Spirit a life-giving source, the Holy Spirit is also a community-building spirit. The Holy Spirit almost always comes in community and the gifts of the Spirit, the fruit of the Spirit, are given not to an individual but they are given to the collective. We have these gifts not for ourselves to lord it over each other, but we have these gifts in the context of the whole for the building of community.

## DEVELOPMENT AS PARTNERSHIP

It is important for us Christians to remember that to whom much is given of them shall much be required by God. Action on behalf of the poor and powerless peoples of the world is action on behalf of those who are continually being created in God's image. Development is the task of collaborating with God in re-creating that image in them. We share a common heritage as God's creatures; we also share the possibilities of a common future in the Kingdom where there will be no more hunger, no poverty, no disease, no injustice.

Development must continue to be for the people and by the people. Democratic ideals have to remain in place. Development is not just about making many rich. Development is about making all people whole. If some people have to be less rich so that all people can enjoy the fullness of life, that is what development and the Gospel are all about. Development is that which involves people in community, not individualistic approaches whether by organizations or by churches, imposing their will on others, but people working together in community. Development is accomplished principally through organization and discipline.

Development is also an indigenous process. It comes from below, up. It never starts from the top and goes down. If it starts from the top, it never reaches the bottom. Never.

Development must also be an integrated process. There are many components that must come together since no one individual, or group of individuals, possesses the total range of resources, insights and circumstances that are required to build community. If it is to be integrated, all sorts of conditions of persons must be involved.

Wayne Bragg, in the International Review of Mission, 1984, offered this definition: "Development that is Christian is transformation of the person and social structures that frees persons and societies to move toward a state of increasing fullness in harmony with God, with themselves, with others, and with the environment."

David Korten, in his very helpful book, Getting To The 21st Century, has also offered some forward thinking in this debate: "The critical development issue for the 1990s is not growth. It is transformation. Our collective future depends on achieving a transformation of our institutions, our technology, our values, and our behavior consistent with our ecological and social realities. This transformation must address three basic needs of our global society."[2] He goes on to name these needs as Justice, Sustainability and Inclusiveness; and sees them as "the defining principles of authentic development." He offers some very powerful guidelines towards engagement in what he called a "people-centered development process."

In its World Development Report 1991, the World Bank revisited the Development debate and chose as its theme for that year: "The Challenge of Development." Its opening words were as follows: "Development is the most important challenge facing the human race. Despite the vast opportunities created by the technological revolutions of the twentieth century, more than 1 billion people, one-fifths of the world's population, live on less than one dollar a day - a standard of living that

Western Europe and the United States attained two hundred years ago. The task is daunting, but by no means hopeless."[3]

In offering some priorities for action, the Report favors what it calls a market-friendly approach to development, including investment in people. The Report asserts that: "Succeeding in development is indeed the most pressing of all the challenges that now confront the human race. Incomplete though our understanding still is, enough has been learned in the past forty years to point the way." We are therefore required as Christians to seek for partnerships in solidarity against the poverty in our world.

We must make a very careful distinction between partnerships as ends in themselves, and partnership as a common instrument to a greater end. There is nothing intrinsically wrong with the former types of partnerships. They only become very boring after a while, they can bring out the worst in us, and they often become self-defeating sooner or later. It is true that they may help to develop more globally-literate citizens, especially in the United States where global illiteracy is not on the decline. It is true that they foster individual friendships across cultural boundaries, while they may also be strengthening local groups in various parts of the world. Yet none of this detracts from the stark fact that a partnership that lives to itself will inevitably die by itself. So we do not need partnerships that merely stay alive, we need partnerships that live to give life to others. The highest compliment that a partnership can receive is that it existed chiefly for the benefit of those who were not necessarily within its fold. The Christian principles of sacrifice and service lie at the very heart of what Jesus and his Gospel were all about.

Partnerships then are not about what we can get, but rather about what we can do together so that others might get, especially those who have nothing. Christian partnerships cannot afford to be self-centered collectives, however enlightened the self-interest might be. They are mandated by the Gospel of Jesus Christ to be coalitions of selflessness, seeking to spend and be spent in fighting the causes of poverty and powerlessness, without fighting against the poor, redressing the inequities of resource scarcity and the mal-distribution of goods and opportunities, calling things by their right names when structures of injustices break the backs of the weak. They are coalitions of genuine concern for the human condition, networking for the poor and oppressed, taking their agenda from the sufferings of the underprivileged, because they are able to see Jesus in the faces of those people. Partnerships are there to empower people to live more simply so that others may simply live. Genuine partnerships do not care about what you have, they are chiefly concerned with who you are. In genuine partnerships, the verb to be is important, the verb to have is not; for there is the basic Christian affirmation that our lives do not consist in the abundance of the things which we possess.

The church is sometimes unwilling to risk becoming the poor church - it prefers to retain the more comfortable status of the "church for the poor." The gospel of pragmatism seldom surrenders to the demands of the Gospel of the Kingdom of God when the concerns of the poor are involved. The church is yet to succeed in encouraging its rich membership to live more simply so that the poor might simply live. We should not, however, underestimate the increasing amount of charitable contributions which churches make to the relief of world poverty. If only the causes of poverty could be structurally dismantled, what a difference these contributions would make!

Accordingly, the church must come to see itself as a global community in solidarity and partnership against all that inhibits the fullness of human liberation and dignity. The church must continue to call into serious question any image of itself, any practice it sanctions, which would essentially challenge the claim that all persons are created in God's own image. The church's vision of God must not only seek to form God's people, but also to transform God's people, in the light of the Gospel of Jesus Christ. Development is about transformation. The Gospel of Jesus Christ, as the good news of change for the better, must also be the mandate for partnership in development. The story of the church in its forward march of history must be like a living active parable, a parable of the Kingdom of God. It must strive to enact new possibilities of human partnerships and relationships so that the hungry, the homeless, and the humiliated might not forever feel their loss of human dignity. The loss of food, shelter, or prestige, is not the loss of life, at least, not yet; but such is not the human condition that we would wish for ourselves. God has not given up on those who suffer such indignities, and neither can the church, if it is to be the church. Redemption is possible, for redemption has already been assured in Christ. It is the joy of the church to resonate with everyone that will challenge faith, inspire hope, and articulate the meaning of love in action.

Can Christian culture be transformed? Can the church become an authentic agency of radical change for the better, for development? Are there grounds for purposeful hope that rabid individualism may yet give way to wholesome forms of common action and Christian solidarity? The following words of Robert Bellah and his colleagues may yet inspire some hope:

> *"Perhaps life is not a race whose only goal is being foremost. Perhaps true felicity does not lie in continually outgoing the next before. Perhaps the truth lies in what most of the world outside the modern West has always believed, namely that there are practices of life, good in themselves, that are inherently fulfilling. Perhaps work that is intrinsically rewarding is better for human beings than work that is only intrinsically rewarded. Perhaps enduring commitment to those we love and civic friendship toward our fellow citizens are preferable to restless competition and anxious self-defense. Perhaps common worship, in which we express our gratitude and wonder in face of the mystery of being itself, is the most important thing of all. If so, we will have to change our lives and begin to remember what we have been happier to forget."*[4]

The thought of civic friendship or common worship in our social ethos can only begin to make sense if we are prepared to risk certain securities and overthrow certain idols of our contemporary culture. Certain myths will have to come alive again; certain moral ideals will need to be revived; certain canons of value and human worth will have to be rediscovered. Can all this really come to pass in a context of such rabid individualism and aggressive competition? America can become what it is often made out to be, namely, a "sweet land of liberty." But the sweetness is not available for all, and the liberty is still a piped dream for many whose umbilical cords are buried here. America is a great country; but it could be even greater. This is the main theme of the next chapter, which takes the form of a sermon delivered in my own congregation at The Holy Comforter Episcopal Church, Washington, D.C., on Independence Day, 1993. Partnership for social change does indeed require collaboration not only between church and state, and head and heart, but also between the strong and the weak, and between peoples of varying walks of faith. It is only through such coalitions that the citadels of hope for a new day of justice can be erected and sustained. To such strongholds for the future then, let us now turn our attention.

# CHAPTER EIGHT

## *Sweet Land Of Liberty*
*"Return to your strongholds O prisoners of hope!"*
*--(Zechariah 9:12)*

Such words bring us great courage, and comfort, and consolation on this special day in our nation's calendar. Today is America's day, July 4th, the day on which we give thanks and celebrate the great historical facts of America. America is a great social experiment that is still being carried out. Two hundred and seventeen years ago, the thirteen states through their representatives, met together and signed the Declaration of Independence, and thus brought into being a new nation. They did it and they made it. For these past 217 years, America has been attempting to work out what that Declaration really meant.

America has been good to so many millions over the years. Yes indeed, as we meet, there is so much to be thankful for. It has fed so many hungry mouths, both within its borders and around the world. It has defended many unprotected peoples around the world. It has charted its courses both on the earth and beyond in outer space. It has rolled back the frontiers of ignorance and created new spheres of knowledge and understanding. It has uncovered new modes of working together; but in the process it has also uncovered new modes of not working together.

America has meant so much to so many. Those of us who were either born here or who have adopted this place as our new home, have all got to acknowledge that there is something good, something special, something unique, about this land which we begin to call great, and which will remain so, and which we hope will be even greater. The land of the free, and the home of the brave!

Yes, in so many ways it is the bread basket for countless mouths, the hope for countless lives and minds, the new Jerusalem for millions outside of it. So there is much to be thankful for in this great land of America. There is much to appreciate, and to respect, and to befriend, about this great land. There is much to promote and to secure about our country, and, in so many ways, we ought indeed to be grateful to God for all that God has done through America for us. So, the fireworks are in order, and the hanging of the flags are in order, and the various means of celebrating this July 4th, are quite in order for we do have much to celebrate and preserve.

Nations rise and fall, and America's fall is yet to come, because America is still on the rise. No civilization lasts forever. So America's turn will come. Certainly not in our lifetime, but it will. In the meantime, we do not look forward to its fall; we look forward to its continued success and rise in greatness, hoping and praying that it will yet become an even greater nation.

So we can afford to be grateful and celebrate it, we can afford to be romantic about this great country, and to sing the national songs. We owe it to ourselves, we owe it to our country we owe it to our history to let our voices be heard, and to celebrate this great historical fact, a fact that could be made even greater. Yes, we can be romantic, but alas, we also need to be realistic. The romanticism that we express today, must also be touched by a reasonable amount of realism, about this great country of America.

I said just now that it is great, but that it could be even greater. Realism strikes us in the face, realism strikes us in the heart, realism is there for those who have eyes to see. We live in a world which some consider to be more dangerous now than it was five years ago. Why? Because five years ago, there were two super-powers, with one intending to cancel out the other. If you know that you have an enemy of whom you are afraid, then you act with circumspection and restraint. You have to be careful what you do, and say, and whom you touch, because if you step on somebody's foot, there is somebody who will step back on yours, with perhaps equal force. That was five years ago. Today, there is only one super-power left, this great country of America.

America has in its hands the power to do anything with anybody, anywhere in the world or in space, and there is no super-power left to say, "No, you don't!" For many people this is not a situation of peace, it is a situation of a greater threat to world peace. Many people think so. So this nation is great but could be even greater. If only it could use the super power it has in a super responsible way! But that is still left to be seen.

Realism has to match our romanticism, because in the midst of all the prosperity, and progress, and wealth, which creates a great historical and global appeal, this great country still suffers from what I choose to call "I" disease. By "I" disease I am not referring to glaucoma, or any other physical malady. I am referring to a set of unfortunate characteristics in its social, political and economic life which begin with the letter "I." It stands in the way of making this great country greater. With this "I" disease America suffers from an overdose of "Impressionism," fighting against truth. Ours is a social ethos, led particularly by the media, and television, and movie screen, where impressions count, but truth does not count as much. Thus both in the public and corporate structures of leadership in this country, it is not how you deal with the truth that counts, but the impression that you give, and what you get people to believe. I call that a part of the "I" disease. What you see, is not really what you get. It seems to be more important to give people a 6 for a 9, than to let them know that they are only getting a 6. Yes, impressions count, but truth does not count as much.

In this "I" disease, the appetite to "Imitate," is far more ferocious, far more consuming than the appetite to create, and to use our creative energies and talents, to do for ourselves, to break new ground for ourselves. America is all overwhelmed by a desire to imitate, to follow the current fashion, to try and step in line with those who have already stepped ahead. We do not wish to be the odd person out, we must be a part of the fashion, we must go with the flow, we must do what others do. Yes, imitation becomes more important than creativity. So that when we must express our creative intelligence, we worry because we are not proud of it, we have no confidence in it. It may get us into trouble, we say, it is easier to do what they are doing, better to be lost in the ecology, to get lost in the crowd, to follow them, to imitate them and remain safe. Yes, this is part of the "I" disease.

Another part of it is a national surge of "Impatience." We in America do not know how to wait. We do not know what it means to wait on others; to give them a chance; just to "give them a break," just a little more time, by just waiting. No! We don't allow time to control us; we own time; we tell time what to do. So we are impatient. The great thing about life is speed, and instancy. We don't want it tomorrow, want it now, for we cannot wait. I am having a hard time in trying to make up my mind about which computer to buy, because I am constantly being told that a new chip is coming out soon, and that it will be much faster than the older chips. Just when I would settle on one chip, somebody tells me to wait awhile because that chip is going out of style. Another chip is being introduced. As it is with the computer, so too with the automobile and the aircraft. President Reagan once spoke of the possibility of a airliner that could fly from Washington to Tokyo in two hours. You need more than a day to transport yourself over into a Japanese culture from American culture! At least you have to practice how to bow properly, and how to use the chopsticks correctly. But there is a great deal of impatience in our culture. You see it in the way we deal with one another; we do not give each other a second chance. You see it in the way we treat our children. Most children no longer have the flexibility of being children anymore, for our children are now making adult mistakes. When we were young we made children's mistakes; but we can't wait for children now to work out their children mistakes. So we are blaming our children, because the mistakes they're making are adult mistakes, and we are not allowing them to be children anymore. Yes, America is suffering from "I" disease called "Impatience," we are in a breathless hurry, to get on. We are losing that sense of maturity, because the process of maturity takes time. It has to set. Relationships have to grow little by little.

America is suffering from the lack of sensitivity as well, from "Insensitivity," or a lack of feeling. If you don't believe me, watch the next time that TV camera has to zoom in on someone who is undergoing some kind of trauma, some pain. As soon as the camera sees one's eyes begin to get a little moist, it focuses on those eyes until the tears come down, because it loves to see people cry, and writhe in pain. Everyone's private business must become public business, regardless of what the children have to do and feel with their friends at school afterwards. What happens to the rest of the family after all their business has been exposed to the public? It doesn't seem to matter. They want news; they want it now; and the only news that really sells, is bad news. So there is more pain, more violence, more dirt, more scandal; and the more the merrier! We want it. We love it. What a great deal of Insensitivity! So there is an absence of social compassion, an absence of being sensitive, a neglect of putting ourselves right into the heart, the homes, the lives of others, to feel what they feel, to understand what they are understanding, and just to give them a chance. No! This is a great nation; this is a powerful nation. It does not answer to anyone. So if you want to be insensitive, that's the name of the game.

Beloved, in this great nation that could be even greater I call these the symptoms of the "I" disease - Impatience, Imitation, Insensitivity and Impressionism. We meet to celebrate and to thank God for this great country of ours. None of us would readily suggest that in some way or another God has not been good to us through the American bounty.

Yes! Let us be thankful; but let us also be realistic. It is a great country that could be even greater, if it would only take its formative documents seriously. Listen to the following document, which was signed on the 4th of July, 217 years ago:

> *"We hold these truths to be self-evident that all men are created equal, that they are endowed by their creator with certain inalienable rights, among these are life, liberty and the pursuit of happiness."*

We hold these truths to be obvious, to be self-evident, nobody can counteract them; nobody can argue with them; these are truths, not impressions, truths. All men are created equal. Presumably to be created means that there is a creator, and the creator is indeed mentioned. We have to assume that the creator to whom they refer is the God of Jesus Christ, the one whom we are worshiping today. That document said that these rights are endowed by the creator: life, liberty and the pursuit of happiness. America has been trying to work out, in so many strange ways, what those inalienable rights really are.

"Life" I suppose has a particular meaning in the document; so too does "Liberty." Let us concentrate for a brief moment on the third one, "the pursuit of happiness." Some legal scholars tell us that the phrase originally meant the right to own property and to have that property protected. When the signers of the Declaration signed that was their basic meaning. But some other scholars go on to suggest that the pursuit of happiness went beyond the business of property. They suggest that it had to do with not only seeking the good for yourself, but also with seeking the common good, the good of the whole. The second and later interpretation is problematic. It seems to get in the way of the earlier interpretation. The first one seems to be alright, doesn't it? The business of property is fundamental because of the principle of law. We must not forget that we are a nation of laws. The central principle of law in this great nation, is not based on the person, it is based upon property. What you have is more important than who you are.

The pursuit of happiness, related more to the verb *to have*, than to the verb *to be*, has all kinds of implications for our social ethos: how we live, how we relate to each other, how we determine the weak from the strong. It also has implications for how we view this great nation, because the pursuers of happiness view America as a land of entitlement. So the greed comes in, the materialism comes in, the selfishness comes in, sometimes what is known as "enlightened self-interest" comes in. The looking out for Number One comes in, because it is a land of entitlement. The most difficult political issue on Capitol Hill (Washington, D.C), year after year, is how much money we ought to spend to help those who are helpless. It is about how much are we taking away from those whom we claim to be entitled to what they have, or to what they can get.

Yes! The pursuers of happiness view this land as a land of entitlement. "Let me get what I can," they say, "let me keep as much of what I have as I can; I don't care what happens to the other person." So entitlement is arranged in all kinds of ways. The healthcare debate in which we are now involved deals with who is entitled to what. The biggest revolution that this country would ever see would be if we were to say that all pensioners would no longer have any pension. The whole country would go up in smoke tomorrow. Entitlement is what you have worked for and what you must get. Therein lies the rough edge, because, in this desire to pursue happiness in this great land of entitlement of all kinds, how much you are really entitled to creates problems of great proportions. But alas, this country that is great could be even greater, because although one of the inalienable rights is the pursuit of happiness, such pursuit of happiness takes place in a context of social and national entitlement.

The signers of the Declaration of Independence ended the document with two very important words. They pledged to each other their resources and commitment, and it ended with two words, "sacred honor." I want to suggest, dear friends, that as we think through what it means to be a part of the American fact ... (since all of us are, none of us can escape) ... as we think through, day by day, what it means to be a part of the American fact, that we move on from seeing ourselves as the pursuers of happiness, and that we also see ourselves as persons of honor. It is there in the document. There is something special, about being a person of sacred honor. Honor comes from the Latin word which also means "dignity," "worth." We speak of human dignity, don't we? We speak of the dignity of the male, the dignity of the female, the dignity of the human person. We also speak of honor, but alas, honor is not something which can be bought in the shops and stores of our cities. Good habit comes from God. It comes from a sense of being an agent of God, a child of God, not just the creature, but the child. One who responds to God, who is the God of honor, is also a pursuer of happiness as well as a person of honor. Honor possesses a sense of truth. Honor is linked inextricably with a sense of justice. Honor carries with itself a sense self-worth and self-esteem. Honor means placing the highest possible premium on one's life, and on the lives of others as well.

To be an honorable person means not only that we value our own selves very highly, but that we give that same value to others also. That is what St. Paul is suggesting, we should give to everyone their due, honor to whom honor is due. To put it in ordinary terms, let us give Jack his jacket!

Thus, one who is a pursuer of happiness, and who is becoming also a person of honor, is a very important person indeed. America then is not only a land of entitlement, it is a land of service. Service, yes, because it is an honorable thing to serve. It is an honorable thing to reach out to others and help them up. Your greatest honor is not in what you are asked for, but in what you make available so that others might live. That is where your honor truly lies.

The Washington Post recently paid a very special tribute to man of whom most of us have never heard. That man was on Pennsylvania Avenue, South East, (Washington, D.C) one afternoon where gas was escaping from an underground pipeline. He saw what was happening and decided to stand nearby in order to warn the oncoming traffic about the possibility of danger in that vicinity. A van which was travelling in the area experienced engine failure in the immediate vicinity; but as the man tried to warn the driver, apparently some spark escaped from the engine and the whole van went up in flames. The man got caught in the flames. He rolled himself over trying to extinguish them; but he was too badly burned, and he died the next day. He was either 51 or 52 years of age, and a picture of himself and his wife appeared on the front page of the Post. The Post carried an editorial, not praising him for his death, but praising him for doing something very valuable even if he had to pay the price for it with his life.

During the past week, a Montel Williams TV Show gathered together unsung heroes; people who had done remarkable and courageous things to help others, risking their lives, but who did not make the headlines in the news. Montel called them in and gave each one of them a plaque of appreciation. They were real heroes who did not make the headlines but who had been of sterling service to others anyway. The show demonstrated in no uncertain way that the land of entitlement can also be a land of service.

Dear sisters and brothers, we need to train our younger ones, not merely by what we say, but also by what they see us do. They must know that we are here to serve others, not just to be served. They must know that it is not entitlement alone that counts, but the desire to be of service, of useful service to others. Even if you retire from your official job, it doesn't mean that God has withdrawn from you the talents, the opportunity, or even the will to be of service to others. Very often I come across many people who do much better after they are retired than when they were working regularly. Let no retired person think that retirement is it; sit back, relax, and therefore have a good time. This should not be so. As long as there is life in our bodies, there is almost always something that we can do. We must never feel within ourselves that there is nothing more that we can do, for this is a land of servicing and we must give and give, and do and do, until it hurts. It is not only the land of entitlement, it is also a land of service, because as we pursue happiness and comfort, we also have the sense of honor to sustain.

There is one other thing, however, and this is where the prophet Zechariah helps us today. Zechariah said to the people of old, *"Return to your stronghold, O prisoners of hope, I declare that I will repay to you double."* Many of us in this country live lives of great ambivalence, great ambivalence about America. We are not so sure if we ought to sing the national songs today. Although we are said to have been created equal, we are not at all sure that the signers of the Declaration really meant that we were equal to them; because their slaves were their property, their prisoners. Most of us here are descendants of those slaves. So we have inherited something of a sense of ambivalence. America is great, but it could be even greater, if only certain things were put in place.

Those of us who are colored, regardless of the lightness or darkness of our complexion, are in some way on the underside of this American fact, yes, the underside. We feel the brunt of America. We feel the pain of America. We bear in our souls the burden of America. We know that we cannot live ordinary human lives. We still have to be on our P's and Q's; all of us, and we all have to be extra careful.

Let me share with you what I mean. I was going into a store the other day with a magazine in my hand. While I was half-way there, I turned back to put the magazine in my car before entering the store. Why did I choose to do this? Because, I said to myself, "I don't want anybody to feel that I was stealing the magazine, although my name is clearly on the address label." Why should I have to be so careful? Often when I go up to the check-out counter in a store, and there is a little white old lady ahead of me with her pocket book on the counter, and she looks back and sees me, she grabs her pocket book and clutches it for safety from me, because my face is black. Or again, I may be walking down the aisle in the supermarket, and the pocket book is opened, they rush to secure the pocket book (purse) because I seem to fit the description of a likely thief. My own son can't tell you the number of times he has tried to enter a shopping mall and has been ushered out only because he is a young black man.

Yes! This country is great, but it could be even greater. Everyone who is black has something of a sense of living in an open prison. It is just a little time before our number comes up, our name is called, and something goes wrong for us. So the prophet Zechariah is asking, if you feel yourself a prisoner, and if you still want to be a pursuer of happiness, and a person of honor, how can you mix being a prisoner with these two qualities. His reply is, *"Become a prisoner of hope, yes, a prisoner of hope; and return to your stronghold of faith; and put yourself in the position where hope means everything for you in spite of the fact that the odds are always against you."*

Yes! There is much racism in this great land, and it is not dying; it is rising. Yes! There is much sexism in this land, our women folk are still having a rough time in realizing for themselves their full personal worth and just rights as human beings. We men are mainly responsible for that. Our women folk are prisoners of their own gender. Yes! There is a great deal of ethno-centrism in this land. A great distinction is made between certain people who look and sound one way, and the others who do not. Yes! There is a great deal of materialism in this land. All of us, in some way or another, are prisoners of these "isms," but the prophet Zechariah says that we can become prisoners of hope, because we are not merely created people, but we are more significantly people created in the image of God. If a country truly belongs to God, then we are all a part of God's loving and creative design.

So we must not be worried. We must keep on keeping on. We must hope that one day poverty will be removed entirely from our midst. We must hope against hope that one day racism will be removed from the face of this planet. We must hope against hope that women will no longer have to be imprisoned in their God-given gender, nor denied their full rights and privileges as full human beings. We must hope against hope that there will truly be equal access, equal opportunity for all, whether or not people have a recognizable name, and not because of a fairy god-mother or fairy god-father on the inside. Yes! This country is great, but it could be even greater.

You and I who are pursuers of happiness, you and I who are trying to be persons of honor, must also be prisoners of hope. We must see this land, not just as a land of entitlement, not just as a land of service, but also as a land of opportunity. We have the time, we have the position, we have the power, and we can make a little go a long way. We must provide the opportunities for others, especially for those who are coming behind, so that they will not have to have it as hard as we have had. But we must be prisoners of hope, working harder and harder to ensure that, as day succeeds day, it is possible for us to sing these great words: "My country 'tis of thee, Sweet land of liberty, Of Thee I sing."

Let me issue one last warning. Because we are prisoners of hope, let us not lull ourselves into a false sense of **success**. Many of us are giving up. We are settling down. We are becoming complacent. We are forgetting the struggles of those who were before us. We still have to build up the structures for those who are coming after us. Let us not lull ourselves into a false sense of success. Yes, the God who has been our help in ages past is still our hope for years to come. That God is to be our shelter from the stormy blast and our eternal home. That can only mean that we are prisoners of hope, and not settling down simply because we have acquired a Cadillac, or a Volvo, or a Buick, or some other fast and fancy car. We have not arrived; none of us has; we are still moving on.

Let us not lull ourselves into a false sense of **security**, for that would be dangerous. The enemy is still at the gate, the pressures and evils of life are still there. We have to be vigilant, we have to be watchful, because our enemy, as a roaring lion still walks about seeking some to devour. We have to resist steadfast in the faith as prisoners of hope.

Finally, let us not lull ourselves into a false sense of **strength**. Yes, we are strong but there may well come someone who is even stronger. Remember that Jesus says that when the strongman armed keeps his house, his goods are safe. But when one stronger than he comes, what does he do? He despoils his goods. So let us not lull ourselves into a false sense of strength. You may feel strong today, but you can be weak tomorrow.

So beloved, let us return to the strongholds of God, let us make sure that as we live out this American fact we live it out as prisoners of hope. Let us remember that as we try to be pursuers of happiness, we must also try to be persons of real honor, prisoners of hope, so that this great land of America, this land of entitlement and of service, can also be a land of opportunity.

*Our fathers' God to thee,*
*Author of liberty,*
*To thee we sing;*
*Long may our land be bright*
*With freedom's holy light;*
*Protect us by thy might*
*Great God our King.*

May God bless everyone of you. Amen.

# CHAPTER NINE

## *THE CHURCH AS COMMUNION: IN FAITH, LIFE AND WITNESS*

The central task of this chapter is to try some peeling of the most popular ecumenical onion of our time, known as "Communion," or "Koinonia," or "Communio;" without allowing the juice to get into our spiritual eyes, or the lingering smell to remain on our denominationally religious fingers. We shall be looking at three of the four basic pillars of our religion - Faith, Life, and Witness. The fourth, I suggest, is Hope. Because we have chosen these three pillars, as the context of our ecumenical search for the common life in the Body of Christ, let us set for ourselves the following question: <u>How can we make Faith the witness in life, while witnessing to the Life of Faith, as living witnesses to the Source of our Faith</u>?

It would certainly be difficult for anyone to deny that we are now going through a very cloudy period in our ecumenical pilgrimage. Many ecumenists and ecumenical officers have in recent times felt as if they have been left holding the bag. Various persons have attempted to put their labels on the present ecumenical climate. For example, it has been referred to as the "winter of ecumenism." Some speak of the obvious decline in ecumenical enthusiasm and commitment to the goals of visible Christian unity. They point to the rise in theological conflict, the new obstacles emerging to growth in communion, the practical difficulties of cashing the checks of theological convergence, the growing crisis of authority in many denominations, and the narrowing of denominational concerns and expectations.

Some would prefer to call it "Ecumenical fatigue." Although Second Isaiah promised that people of hope would run and not be weary, he did not promise that they would not grow old. The fatigue has increased, because most participants in the ecumenical movement have tended to make it more of a hundred-yard sprint, rather than a long-distance relay race; and there is a pitiful scarcity of runners to take over the batons falling around us one by one.

Others would perhaps want to refer to it as a period of "Ecumenical Recession." They would posit that such was inevitable, since the world of the rich has been experiencing an economic recession. The point here is that the history of the ecumenical movement in this century has been inextricably tied up with the history of those countries and communities that could afford to pay for it, almost as a form of exotic and extra-curricular religious activity. This is further strengthened by the observation, that the history of the ecumenical movement in countries and communities that could not afford to pay is bound up with their ability to get it paid for by others.

There has been no substantive ecumenism without the spending of large sums of money, and the decrease of ecumenical activity has been somewhat directly related to the increased unavailability of funds to support it. Rich churches are finding it hard to stay afloat themselves, and therefore increasingly harder to keep the ecumenical movement afloat with its accustomed styles and symphonies. If the ecumenical movement is to survive in any shape or form, it will have to learn how to do things radically differently, regionally, nationally and globally; especially how to do much more with much less.

Let us never forget that, apart from the Resurrection appearances, the only other miracle story reported in all four New Testament Gospels is the feeding of the five thousand with a few loaves and two fish. Maybe this is a time to rediscover what the Early Church meant by using that as its anchor story in the public ministry of Jesus. Many ecumenical officers not only function on shoe-string budgets; they have the strings, but they have no shoes. It may well be that their new role will be to teach the rest of the church how to do ministry without shoes, or staff in the hand, or purse. On the other hand, ecumenical officers will need to become more aggressive in getting their churches to share the poverty more equitably throughout, rather than sit by and wring their hands, and allow themselves and their programs to be chopped off under the official excuse of fiscal constraints.

Ecumenism has also been overtaken by the politics of inclusiveness. Many Christians around the world have still not recovered from the World Council of Churches Canberra Assembly of 1992, which has been referred to as a "contentious gathering," a restless assembly, which admitted its own "failures of understanding, sensitivity and love." Old hierarchies, old dynasties and hegemonies have been eroded. Cherished domains and privileges have evaporated. New forms of coalition have been forging ahead. Cultural pluralism has become a fact that can no longer be quietly ignored or respectfully silenced. Theological discourse now takes place in many more languages and images than before. Persons who believe differently are commanding greater attention than those who claim to share the same faith. In other words, the politics of inclusiveness is putting a new spin on the meaning of "Communion" itself, and the steady surge towards new forms of diversity in religious and social life has derailed many dearly held notions of ecumenism.

What are we to make of all these analyses and descriptions of the current ecumenical climate - "Winter," "Decline," "Fatigue," "Recession," "New Inclusiveness?" Are they really indicative of the ecumenical spirit of the age, or are they mere symptoms of a type of malaise which really does not affect the true fabric of our faith, life and witness? If we continue to speak of the ecumenical movement as a pilgrimage, could it be that it is really a celestial pilgrimage, moving through the skies, passing through spots of turbulent cloudiness, but still firmly fixed on course, with its compass unadjusted, and its divine radar picking up clearer patches and smoother air further along the way? Or should we be prepared for a bumpy ride all the way, trying to discern more clearly, though painfully, that following Jesus as the Way, the Truth, and the Life, truly involves taking up the Cross daily, and learning the lessons of discipleship through the ecumenical school of hard knocks? Or should we borrow a line from President Clinton in his Inaugural Speech (1993), when he said that "deep in the midst of winter we force the spring?" Which ever image we use, it is clear to me that this transitional era in ecumenism is both inevitable and necessary. It provides us with a door of opportunity, so that we might be emancipated from the bondage of some of our ecumenical mistakes and denominational memories, and be swept up by the rushing mighty winds of God's convulsive Spirit, who blows where God wills, without Agreed Statements, Concordats, or Ecumenical Assemblies.

## *Communion How?*

The multiplicity of ecumenical dialogues has created a remarkable consensus about the dominant theme in ecclesiology. In spite of the fact that the New Testament has given strong expression to several different tasks of the church, as inherent in the proclamation of the Gospel of Jesus Christ - tasks such as Service, Healing, Edification, Teaching, Worship, and so forth, ecumenical dialogue has nailed its hopes for unity to the mast of Communion, or Koinonia. It is said that "this is the reality which those various New Testament images bring to manifold expression." (Faith & Order Paper 156, p.46) In doing so, it has elevated this single task beyond the status of the others, and it has endowed it with divine significance and universal appeal. The preoccupation with "Communion" has so given rise to a kind of ecumenical psychosis, that we are now in danger of becoming immune to what it can really do for us in our common search for the answer to the most urgent question of our time. That question is: **What does it take to live the Christian life in the modern world?** This is the underlying and most integrative question about Faith, Life, and Witness. There are ecumenical dimensions to the answer, yes, but there are also diakonal, political, liturgical, ethical and cultural dimensions as well.

The Canberra Assembly had declared that "the unity of the Church to which we are called is a koinonia given and expressed in the common confession of the apostolic faith; a common sacramental life entered by the one baptism and celebrated together in one eucharistic fellowship; a common life in which members and ministries are mutually recognized and reconciled; and a common mission witnessing to the gospel of God's grace to all people and serving the whole creation." (Faith And Order Paper, No. 157, p.86) Actually, Canberra was not saying anything new, for the whole grammar of the ecumenical movement had been focussing on these elements for decades. Common confession, mutual recognition, and common structures have always been seen as the foundations of visible Christian unity in WCC language. However, Canberra goes further to speak of koinonia as "given and expressed" in certain terms.

It is this phrase - "given and expressed" - which perhaps underlines the difficulties surrounding the notion of Communion, for there is a presumption that true communion can only be expressed in visible unity. But no collective enduring notion of visible unity exists, this is because of the ontological realities of diversity inherent in God's created order. Further, to speak of Communion as given begs the question of the giver. To speak of Communion as given by God is to speak of God as Spirit, and that is precisely where diversity rules. The Roman Catholics and Methodists in their 1991 Joint Report had this to say:

> *"The Spirit distributes gifts to all for the good of the koinonia (1 Cor. 12:1-11). The Spirit is the inner power of the new life in Christ. Because the faithful are in Christ and with Christ, they receive the Spirit and are in the Spirit. There is a diversity of gifts, yet these are united in their source, the one Spirit, and in their purpose, the koinonia. Yet the Spirit 'blows where it will,' and the faithful cannot put limits to the Spirit's action in humankind."*[1]

We have often sung in our churches that God moves in a mysterious way, God's wonders to perform. We certainly know what we mean, for we continue to worship and believe in a God of surprises. We are reluctant to admit it, but God also works in a very messy way, in very untidy and apparently irreconcilable patterns. Indeed, there is more compelling reason to advance the hypothesis that the atheists are right and that the theists are wrong. Yet central to the genre of our faith, life and witness as Christians, is that we continue to believe in spite of decreasing evidence to justify such belief, both within the community of faith and beyond. Every pastor has heard the story of Farmer Jones. When Pastor Smith complimented him for keeping such a beautiful garden, and tried to give the praise to God for being so good to Farmer Jones, Farmer Jones replied, "Ha! You should have seen this place when God had it all to himself!" There is nothing about our experience of divine creativity so far that should lead us to suggest that the God of Moses, and the God whom Jesus of Nazareth called Father, was ever self-disclosed in an ordered, tidy and unified way. The challenge of the biblical tradition has always consisted not so much in looking for God in similarities and matching forms, but much more in identifying the hand and Spirit of

God in widely differing events and unlikely circumstances. Cyrus of Persia is God's "Messiah," God's anointed one. The Son of God is born in a stable. The landless slaves of Egypt become God's elect. Women become the first witnesses of the Empty Tomb. A Roman centurion becomes a living paradigm of faith. The reign of God is validated on a cross and not in a palace. The supreme miracle of Resurrection, that most formative fact for Christian faith, is devoid of any actual witnesses, so that the unity of the faith might be in the God who performed it, rather than in the diverse people who have believed it down through the ages.

There is another side to God's disruptive and untidy forms of revelation. It is found in Jesus himself. In his beatitudes, and in his proclamation of the reign of God, (as that which neither comes with observation nor fits any human design) Jesus not only seeks to change the terms of reference about what is acceptable with God, but he also celebrates the inherent worth and dignity of the least of the socially respected. People of faith are people of faith because they see things differently from the prevailing norms. "To you is given to know the mystery of the reign of God, but to others everything is done in riddles," he says. Mary Magdalene and Judas Iscariot become persons of significance during his ministry, even if one fails him in the end. He overturns the table of money-changers in the Temple, not so much as a revolutionary act, but rather as an acted parable to demonstrate his understanding of who God is and what God wants. God wants wrong things made right, even if structures have to be radically transformed, and seemingly immovable obstacles have to be dissolved. For the vitality of the community of faith, the koinonia, consists not in what is seen, but rather in how things are seen, and in how the common sharing of the same Gospel addresses the world with transforming effect and liberating result. For the things which are seen are said to be temporal, but the things which are not seen, but yet wholly felt, are eternal.

I am increasingly convinced that part of our dilemma in the world of ecumenical dialogue and reconstruction has come about because we have left undone some of the things we ought to have done earlier, and we have done those things which we ought not to have done so soon; and there is less health in us. We have spent an inordinate period of time trying to get our Ecclesiology straightened out, and we have not. We have spent an equally amount of time carving out a common Christology and it has not stuck for any length of time, for christologies are by nature theological models and images with rapidly multiplying effects, second only to pneumatologies. It seems to me that we have not followed through on much of the mandate bequeathed to us by the early pioneers of the ecumenical movement in the early part of this century. We have not wrestled patiently enough, or long enough, with our Missiology.

Why is this so? I believe that it has much to do with the historical manifestations of that five-letter word, P-O-W-E-R. The history of missions in the last century, and in the earlier decades of this one, has shown us that to be in mission often meant being engaged in extending one's range of power and influence, in spreading one's religious ambiance and cultural ethos as far as possible. Mission was essentially the extension of power rather than the transfer of power. It was founded mainly on a principle of extension of the collective self, and therefore on a plerosis, a filling out. It lacked much of the self-emptying praxis of faith, the kenosis, from the Crucified Christ whom they proclaimed. But the world has changed, and the once weak are not that weak any more; the once primitive peoples of the world are more enlightened and self-confident; but they have not beaten the mission of God into retreat, they have continued to take it seriously. On the other hand, the heirs of the traditional pioneers of the mission, having been robbed of a sense of power in Missiology, have now sought refuge in Ecclesiology, hoping to find it there. But find it they will not; for all the power has already been taken by the One who remains real but invisible. The Ecclesia, the Church, is a communion, yes, but it is mystical, and not imperial. "All power has been given to me in Heaven and on Earth," he says, "So don't bother about it; the gates of Hell shall not prevail."

The Lord of the Church is the One who is already on the way towards us, the One who calls us, sends us, empowers us, and sustains us. It is that God who explains to us, *"I will build my Church. Go therefore and preach the Gospel, make disciples, feed my sheep, and do not forget that I am always with you. What more visible unity do you want? Can you not see the same Me in all the sheep that you try to feed, and in your fellow feeders as well? He that hath eyes to see, let him see."* This is the Gospel mandate which demands a life of faithful obedience, courageous self-emptying, and loyal witness. This is the Divine Mission that contains it own koinonia.

## Communion Where?

Ecumenism is not about posturing for Unity, it rather about living out that Unity which is already there, given to us by the Spirit of God, and without need of any validation or certification by council, creed or canon, however much we fail to find appropriate ways of commonly expressing it. So communion is more about partaking than about participation; and this is why koinonia is a word that is both divine and dangerous, disturbing to the status quo.

To explore some of the recent debate about koinonia in ecumenical circles we shall take a look the Final Report of the First Anglican\Roman Catholic International Commission (ARCIC I).[2] We will later make a brief comparative analysis between koinonia in ARCIC I and communion in ARCIC II. Some speak about a koinonia ecclesiology emanating from the Final Report, but we ought also to recognize that there is a koinonia pathology contained within it, which requires urgent analysis. This is even more urgent when we take into account the protracted manner in which both the Anglicans and Roman Catholics have responded to the Final Report.

When I speak of a koinonia pathology, I am referring to a diagnosis of a specific piece of theology rather than to a diagnosis of specific theologians. The diagnostic approach is critically important because the theology under review is the product of a convergence of Scripture, Tradition, Culture, Context, Ideology, and Institutionalism.

In the Introduction of the Final Report, ARCIC I claimed that its search for solutions to the issues which divided us was to take place in our common inheritance, particularly in the Scriptures. It then proceeded immediately to assert that: "Fundamental to all our Statements in the concept of koinonia (communion)."[3] It said that koinonia is the term "that most aptly expresses the mystery underlying the various New Testament images of the Church," although it had already acknowledged two significant things. First, the Church is a mystery which Christians from the beginning have sought to understand. Second, the New Testament never equates the term "Church" with the term koinonia. Yet the ARCIC I members affirmed that "Koinonia with one another is entailed by our koinonia with God in Christ. This is the mystery of the Church." They went on to state that "the koinonia is grounded in the word of God preached, believed and obeyed. Through this word the saving work of God is proclaimed."[4]

Nothing can be said to refute the divines in what they say. However, the pathology lies in what they do not say, and in what they try to do with Koinonia, thereby failing to be radically faithful to the New Testament as a common inheritance. The pathology lies in retreating from the more common use of the verb in the New Testament towards the less used noun. The pathology lies in attempting to speak in definitive terms of church as a mystery already understood, in terms of one paradigmatic word. The New Testament is very consistent in describing how the church works, rather than in offering definitional images for it. The Pauline term "Body of Christ," for example, is a functional phrase, not a static image. The pathology lies in looking for "images" of the Church in the New Testament, rather than in pointing to the many a diverse tasks of the Church which are far more obvious and dynamically significant. Images lay the groundwork for an ecclesiology of models, defined, controlled, and led by those who shape them. So for example, episcope becomes a more immediate outgrowth of koinonia in ARCIC I rather than discipleship. Tasks, on the other hand, give the impetus for common action and witness, for common hope and active mutuality. If therefore we are to retain the centrality of koinonia as the Greek equivalent for "communion" in the New Testament, we will need to treat communion more as activity than as state.

The ARCIC I pathology is further complicated by the notion of visibility, with respect to sacrament, sign, instrument and communion. Koinonia is said to require visible expression in terms of the Church's sacramental nature. Then visible unity is said to be required, since unity is of the essence of the church. This is the argument for full visible communion between Rome and Canterbury. The notion of the Church as a mystery disappears, and the implicit alignment of koinonia with unity now becomes explicit. Thus we hear the ARCIC I divines speaking about preserving a fruitful diversity within the koinonia of local churches, and unity in essentials "which must mark the universal koinonia."[5] Yet at the same time we find them calling for the need to maintain "the just diversity of the koinonia of all the churches."[6]

What does all this have to do with the Church As Communion? How does the koinonia pathology, which I have just been describing, interfere with the post-ARCIC ecclesiology? What happens to the whole Church of God after all the responses are in to all the agreed statements? Let us must make no mistake about it, neither communion is ever going to respond to any ARCIC initiative with any degree of desire for radical change. There is enough evidence to suggest that the ARCIC work-permit was for a process of affirmation, but not for transformation. The ARCIC Minutes in both commissions would tell a story which the Agreed Statements would never disclose. Suffice it to say that koinonia without transformation is no koinonia at all.

So we may well ask the question: how will ecumenism in the 21st century find its new thrust after the inevitable anemia of the late 20th century? Did ARCIC II help to prepare the way? Did its two Agreed Statements, Salvation And The Church (1986)[7], and Church As Communion (1990)[8], help to sort out much of the ARCIC pathology about koinonia? The significant difference between both commissions was only in their composition, there was a wider membership on ARCIC II in terms of ethnic, theological, ideological and geographical distribution. I had the privilege of serving as one of the Archbishop of Canterbury's representatives on ARCIC II for about eight years (1983-1991).

Yet ARCIC II did in fact contribute two documents in eight years to the living memory of our two communions. Salvation And The Church actually fell somewhat outside of our mandate, but it was in response to a specific request from the Anglican Consultative Council, that the doctrine of justification be dealt with before anything else. In my view, this delayed the specific ARCIC II mandate by four years, and significantly affected the whole ecumenical momentum for theological discourse and ecumenical reconstruction. ARCIC II had four specific tasks: Responses to the Final Report; Mutual Reconciliation of Ministries; Moral Issues; and Growth towards Communion. Much of the koinonia pathology of ARCIC I survived in ARCIC II, and "communion" had a very difficult time in settling down with pluriformity and contextuality; and we therefore developed an annual production rate of 10.25 paragraphs between 1983 and 1990.

How then does our second Agreed Statement, Church As Communion, help to prepare us for the next century, especially as we would be well advised to give up this century as a pre-dress-rehearsal for the real performance yet to come? All of the ARCIC work up to this point was said to have "contributed to progress in mutual understanding and growing awareness of the need for ecclesial communion." This last statement was therefore intended to reflect "more explicitly upon the nature of communion and its constitutive elements."[9] We attempted to make communion more of an action word by giving the entire notion a comprehensive significance. We said that "communion embraces both the visible gathering of God's people and its divine life-giving source." And we also said that "communion involves rejoicing with those who rejoice and being in solidarity with those who suffer and those who search for meaning in life. To explore the meaning of communion is not only to speak of the Church but also to address the world at the heart of its deepest need, for human beings long for true community in freedom, justice and peace and for the respect of human dignity."[10]

We then proceeded to discuss the broad theme of Communion in terms of Scripture, Sacramentality and the Church, Apostolicity, Catholicity and Holiness, Unity and Ecclesial Communion, and Communion between Anglicans and Roman Catholics. What happened to good old koinonia? You will notice what we said in Para.12. We said that it was a word which tied together a number of basic concepts "such as unity, life together, sharing and partaking." We emphasized the verbal form first, as meaning to share, participate, have part in, have something in common, or act together; while the noun could signify fellowship or community. Thereafter koinonia is never mentioned again. A new pathology begins. We place a very heavy load on the function of the word "communion," as we try to work out, in the areas I have already outlined, what the implications can be for two ecclesial bodies which are truly prepared to take communion seriously.

It can be noticed in the text that there is considerable variety in the way in which the word "communion" is used. We set a new record in the range of phrases on communion. We speak of ecclesial communion, existing communion, Christ's communion with the Father, profound communion, fullness of communion, communion of the Church, communion of those who confess Jesus Christ, communion of love, our present communion with God, communion among those entrusted with the episcopal ministry, communion of all the churches, mutual communion, life in communion with Christ, communion with other local churches, communion in the one Spirit, spiritual communion, visible communion of the Church, communion between bishops, deeper communion with God, full communion, communion founded upon the saving life and work of Christ, communion in both kinds, fuller communion, degree of communion, Anglican Communion, fuller communion for which we strive. That gives us 26 different ways. That is why we can make a boast of ourselves in this sentence: "Developments in the understanding of the theology of communion in each of our churches have provided the background for the Commission's reflections on the nature of communion." (para.55)

It should also be noticed that there is a very sparse attention to the centrality of the Covenant in our common inheritance of Scripture. Apart from the references in paras. 7 and 8, there is no attempt made to flesh out a covenant theology, as say in the COCU theology in this country. The absence of stronger emphasis on the covenant robs us of the more centrifugal approach to an ecclesiology that is marked by the character of God who is encountered in human history. For me, a covenantal theism, a thoroughgoing explication of what is meant in Scripture that the God of Moses and the God of Jesus is encountered in a relationship of bargains and responsibility, makes for a far more dynamic ecclesiology. It makes the centrality of the Eucharist more a matter of common life in the Spirit of Christ, than a determination of apostolic episcope.

Covenantal theism would have enabled us to take ourselves more seriously when we said that exploring communion also meant addressing "the world at the heart of its deepest need." We would also have followed up more faithfully on what we said in para.22: "Confessing that their communion signifies God's purpose for the whole human race, the members of the Church are called to give themselves in loving witness and service to their fellow human beings." It is this sentence which constitutes the critical element for the Church, in spite of the fact that we in ARCIC II have played around with communion in so many terms and phrases.

We urgently need an ecumenism that not only takes human diversity as God's salvific mosaic, but also takes human need and pain as God's primary salvific focus. For there can be no greater risk than in the area of human diversity and human pain, and our ecumenical task is to ensure that our churches find their true communion in what they do together in these critical areas, and not in what they publish together. Our principal focus as agents of Christian Unity should be on organic ecumenism, rather than on structural ecumenism; for communion offers hope for the former, but radically disrupts any efforts towards the latter. Organic ecumenism is about the primacy of divine love and the mystery of its manifestations. Structural ecumenism is about the primacy hierarchical power and universality of its implementation.

The purpose of communion for the church is always to seek to discover the meaning of communion in the world beyond the church, within the context of pluriformity and diverse contextuality, which is given to us by the Spirit of Christ. This is why para.36 is so powerfully demonstrative of what communion entails. It reads in part: "Throughout its history the Church has been called to demonstrate that salvation is not restricted to particular cultures. This is evident in the variety of liturgies and forms of spirituality, in the variety of disciplines and ways of exercising authority, in the variety of theological approaches, and even in the variety of theological expressions of the same doctrine. These varieties complement one another, showing that, as a result of the communion with God in Christ, diversity does not lead to division; on the contrary, it serves to bring glory to God for the munificence of his gifts."

The unity which the Spirit gives is not a unity in form but a unity of essence, and that is itself a mystery over which no human organization can dare preside or assume unrivalled hegemony. Factors of internal organizational discipline and control must never become confused with the essential unity which is ours in Christ, and the task of communion is not to count how many marbles we have, but how those marbles are to be pitched in the game of human history. It is God's game, not ours, and communion is the means whereby we continue to discover what the rules are, and see how far we can pitch. The Church as communion is a living, actualizing, promising, message-bearing, witnessing, suffering, pilgrimage of Christ-confessants, whose only reality consists in their relentless desire to become who they are already. They are a community of saints striving occasionally to be saintly, but never completely abandoning the vocation to which they have been called in the One Lord, One Faith,

One Baptism.

It is this One Baptism which seems to me be so inescapable in our efforts to be truly Christian. It becomes central to the post-ARCIC era, and its centrality is already hinted at in Church As Communion in a way which ARCIC II did not fully acknowledge. But let us trace this through the focus on the Eucharist. The Windsor Statement of 1971 of ARCIC I had spoken of the central place of the Eucharist in the life of the Church: "The identity of the Church as the body of Christ is both expressed and effectively proclaimed by its being centred in, and partaking of, his body and blood".[11] Later on, the Moscow Statement between Anglicans and Orthodox in 1976 had given the Eucharist a place of central significance: "The Church celebrating the Eucharist becomes fully itself; that is koinonia, fellowship - communion. The Church celebrates the Eucharist as the central act of its existence, in which the ecclesial community, as a living reality confessing its faith, receives its realization."[12] Salvation And the Church virtually extended Windsor and Moscow by affirming that "the eucharist is the repeated sacrament by which the life of Christ's body is constituted and renewed, when the death of Christ is proclaimed until he comes again." (Para.16)

With Church As Communion, however, this central focus was significantly altered, and it was clear that the fundamental reality of the Church was that of Baptism, and that the function of the Eucharist was to signify that universal diversity of the baptized, while searching for solidarity with humanity as a whole. This is a major step forward in treating communion as verbal function, in terms of partaking of something, rather than as a participation in a perceived reality. Paras: 36-37 said this in part:

> "At every eucharistic celebration of Christian communities dispersed throughout the world, in their variety of cultures, languages, social and political contexts, it is the same one and indivisible body of Christ reconciling divided humanity that is offered to believers. In this way the eucharist is the sacrament of the Church's catholicity in which God is glorified. In the eucharist the Church also manifests its solidarity with the whole of humanity."

We must come to understand communion therefore as an active reality and not as an imagined condition. The Church is a communion, and not simply like a communion.

This is the challenge which should consume our efforts as we seek to wrestle, not between ourselves with our scandalous and irreconcilable clash of ecclesiologies, but rather cooperatively, with the imperatives of an appropriate faith, life, and witness in a world that already has its own clash of communions anyway. This is the world that we love so dearly, in spite of our confessions to the contrary.

## The Clash Of Communions

What then is this "clash of communions" in our contemporary world? And how does it impact on our own search for the communion inherent in the Divine Mission of salvation? First, there is a clash of communions between Sin and Salvation. The structures of Sin are firmly entrenched in the social and moral fabric of our post-modern culture. Individualism, Materialism, Sexism, Pragmatism, and Racism are not only the ingredients of the glue that holds the communion of Sin together, but they are also the non-negotiable basis on which the terms of Salvation are being offered to the world by us who are supposed to be the communion of saints. The battle for the soul of the world is still being waged with these five pillars of human bondage very much in place.

Second, there is the clash of communions between Bad News and Good News. The tastes and styles of our cultural appetites have given pride of place to the attractiveness of the cruel, the vicious, the sensational, and the obscene. The demonic in our entertainment and communications culture is no longer the "printer's devil" or the "computer virus;" it is rather the common thirst for the absolute worst. Bad news sells well and travels far, and the world finds instant and effective communion in its diffusion. On the other hand, proclamation in the communion of the Good News, the Gospel, is often compromised, intimidated, and muted, because many of its bearers have unwittingly surrendered much of their moral substance and authentic meaning to the values of the other side. Thus Good News is not all that good; and Bad News is not only good for the common heart but also soothing for the guilty conscience.

Third, there is the clash of communions between the Words (the "-ologies") and the Spirit. Our post-modern ethos has made it mandatory that everything of value has to be codified into a science; a recognizable, measurable, and verifiable package of information and technology, by which human existence should be guided, and the meaning of human livelihood should be assessed. I call this the communion of the Words, in which the ineffable becomes unreal, the unscientific becomes unwise, and the untouchable becomes untrue. The communion of the Spirit finds itself vastly overwhelmed, for the traditional claims of transcendent reality, of sacramental vitality, and of spiritual superiority, have all been taken hostage within the communion itself, and the would-be champions of religious and moral supremacy are themselves searching for their own "words," their own "-ologies" to validate their cause.

Fourth, there is the clash of communions of the Past and of the Future. The communion of the Past is the dominance of power and prosperity which has always had the balance of goods and services, of privilege and prominence, of strength and security, swinging mightily in its favor. This is the communion that speaks of the good old days, the pristine era of good old American values, when all was pretty much right with the world. This is the communion that struggles, through its modern cults and movements, its political action committees and philanthropic largesse, its ecclesial agents and intellectual activists, to ensure that not only does the status quo remain intact and inviolate, but that the presumed glories of the past are renewed for greater effectiveness in the future. For them, change is good, provided that things which worked well in the past are simply repaired for more work in the future. In the meantime, the communion of the Future continues to speak about the meaning of heaven as an earthly experience, about bringing in the reign of God as a concrete and historical reality; about transformation of the present in the light of God's liberation, peace and justice which we seek; and about the radical dissolution of the factors which inhibit the flowering of the Age of Fulfillment. But still the marginalized and oppressed, the victims of despair and discrimination, often find themselves caught in the cross-fire between these two communions, and they know not their true friends from their real enemies.

Fifth, there is the clash of communions between the order of Structure and the hope of Freedom. The communion of Structure lays great stress on the need for dogma and discipline, for law and process, for organization and control. It makes human frailty and vulnerability the basis of its order, and it subsists in defining for society the limits and objects of its existence. The communion of Freedom reaches forward into the world of structures, and seeks to redefine humanity in terms of divine grace, and of such attributes as are inherent in being made "in the image and likeness of God." It seeks to confront the other communion with the protest that structures were made for humans and not humans for the structures. But, like the famous credit card advertisement, most humans prefer not to leave home without them. Thus we are stuck with looking for visible unity in our ecumenical search, precisely because we are unable to make better use of the freedom which has already been won for us in Christ through the Spirit of God, who is the very essence of unstructuredness.

These clashes to which we have just referred are deeply rooted in the conscious experience and fertile expectations of our contemporary world. They give life and excitement to the conventions of our times, and they find widespread expression in the very life and culture of our churches. We preach against them on Sundays, but sustain them for the rest of the week. We make our living by them. We heat and cool our churches with them. We construct our policies and make our decisions with them in mind. We use them as paradigms for promotion and preferment, and we try to ignore them when they are brought forcefully to our attention. These are the clashes in our moral culture which we love to hate; and yet, because they speak so loudly to our consciences, we dare not pretend that they do not help us to shape our own image of the God we claim to love, with heart, and mind, and soul, and strength. This is the real communion that we have now. How far does it differ from the koinonia that we seek, in Faith, in Life, and in Witness?

## TOWARDS THE NEW COMMUNION

The World Conference of Faith anf Order, which was held in Santiago, Spain, in

1993, focussed its attention on the theme of Communion in four sections. These were:

> i.  Communion in the one apostolic faith;
> ii. Communion in a shared life in Christ;
> iii. Communion in common witness;
> iv. Future steps towards full _koinonia_ so that the world may believe.

An early draft of its Working Document had issued this challenge: "Before God, each community has to examine itself in order to discover how far it is satisfied with the actual situation, how far it fears to be challenged by everything unity requires of it, how far it prefers to remain enclosed in its own denominational identity, how far visible unity is really a task it is prepared joyfully and confidently to embrace." (April 1992, Para.19) The Document called for a deepening of the degree of communion in apostolic faith and life; but it went on to warn about the "risk that uncontrolled diversity will endanger what has already been achieved" without such a deepening. This constitutes for me a shift from the "unity-in-diversity" theories, with their mechanisms of definition and control, to the "community-through-diversity" experience, with its freshness of charismal grace and ecclesial freedom, although the Document does not say so.

This "Community-through-diversity" experience is perhaps the major antidote to much of what has so far hindered many attempts to break down the walls of division erected by groups of Christians for the preservation of their own sense of safety, sanctity, and control. It confronts the attitudes of intransigence in denominational power and traditions, and it chips away mightily at the structures of fear and resistance to change which dominate the mentality of most of our official church leadership. _Koinonia_ takes on new meaning through this optic, and the realities of what the Church is about, in all its diversity, are no longer solely confined to the traditional images and metaphors we find in the New Testament.

Thus would we offer ourselves, our souls and bodies, as a living sacrifice to the Church, and the whole Church as the new Community.

It is the _Community of believers_, not just a community of faith; because faith is non-existent without human agents. The Working Document stated that "the foundation of our common life is the one God in whom we believe." (Para.38) Perhaps we might be more true to ourselves to say that our common life is founded in a common belief in the one God, to whose call we seek to respond differently.

It is the _Community of Earthen Vessels_, with all the inherent fragility and limited capacity which this entails. Yet this is also the community of charisms, the community in which God's _charismata_, God's spiritual gifts, are acknowledged, treasured, and made available to the world. It is because of this that we struggle in our common weaknesses to avoid handling sacred things with clumsy hands.

It is the _Community of Friends_, in which the most cohesive factor lies in following of the One who laid down his life for his friends, and who calls them friends because they do what he commands, and who love one another because he has commanded them to do so. To live in the community of friends demands that the many factors of friendship be addressed. These obviously involve complementarity, patience, mutual respect, openness, inter-dependence, vulnerability, self-giving, personal clarity, maturity, solidarity, accountability, faithfulness, compassion, and the search for equality. The Church, as a community of friends, must learn to love as friends, and not to live as aliens.

It is the Community of Suffering, which holds up the Cross of the Crucified One as the central historical symbol of God's redeeming love, and our most energizing hope. Poverty and Powerlessness are marks of Jesus on the Cross, so too is his outsiderness. To address the world at its deepest level is to take on suffering and to transform it, making it both a factor for liberation and wholeness as well as a means of overcoming the systemic violence of all our life-styles and institutions.

To be a community of suffering is to bear the marks of Jesus on the body, and Christianity is the most incarnational of all religions. There can be no doctrine of the real presence of Christ in any sacramental or mystical form which does not take the pain and suffering of humanity very seriously, groan with it, writhe with it, fight through it against the pain-makers, and see the hope for relief and liberation bursting forth ever so slowly as the stone is rolled away from the tomb in the world's well kept garden. This is Ecumenism at its heart, this is Christian unity at its best; for we are all joined together as sharers in the pain of humanity. More importantly, the love of Christ constrains us, and we feel it even more than others. Yet it is the suffering together with Christ which even now assures each one of us that we will one day somehow reign together with him.

It is also the Community of Pilgrims; moving forward, ever forward, towards the goal of the prize of the high calling in Jesus Christ; leaving behind the unnecessary baggage of denominational bondage and irreconcilable memories; and reaching forth to such new forms of regenerate life which now seem so untenable and menacing for our traditions, styles and preferred tastes. It is this experience of pilgrimage which more than any other should continue to inform and shape the tone and texture of our ecumenical life, as we seek to discern fresh ways of believing, living and witnessing together, as fellow-travellers on God's highway.

Such pilgrimage requires a fresh readiness for us to be open to new ways of doing things, a readiness to act ourselves into new ways of reflection, articulation and proclamation. Let me, therefore, bring this discussion to a close by offering some proposals for a theological shift in our common dialogue and ecumenical exploration. I wish to suggest that if we are theologically courageous enough to give these proposals a try, we may well be along the way to finding a most appropriate and illuminating answer to our basic question stated earlier: "How can we make Faith the witness in Life, while witnessing to the Life of Faith at the same time, as living witnesses to the Source of our Faith?"

One. Let us shift from an emphasis on cultic transcendence in our working understanding of the doctrine of God to a strengthening of our sense of God's missional condescendence, of our sense of being sent by a God, who also accompanies us, into all the messiness of our world.

Two. Let us begin to take the common engagement in Sin more seriously, not by doing more of it, nor by seeking to compare confession lists in our ecumenical consultations; in other words, not by looking for points of convergence. But let us shift to an emphasis on common repentance, helping each other to understand more deeply and corporately the structural and complex nature of Sin, and also the meaning and measure of God's forgiveness, and offering to the wider world community a clearer line of demarcation between vice and virtue.

Three. Let us make a shift in our ecumenical cosmology. We have been preoccupied with how the world sees us as Christians, and we have been wrestling with notions of visible unity, in order that the world might believe. Our shift must be towards a unity of vision, a common moral vision, towards how we see the world, as we try to re-engage ourselves collectively in God's work of re-creation and redemption. Ecclesiastical window-dressing for the world to see us is substantially different from an authentic ecumenical engagement in the world for God's sake and the Gospel's, towards its liberation and salvation.

Four. Let us return to the patient and diligent study of the Bible together, as a major source of our trying once again to understand the will of God for us. We need more corporate Bible studies at the local ecumenical level, almost at the base-community level, devoid of denominational formularies or clerical gurus. Let us make the shift from treating the Bible as the answer to the world, to listening to God, and seeking God's help in trying to shape the right questions, through a prayerful study of its pages.

Five. If we return to the Bible not so much as the written word of God, but rather as the point where God meets us afresh in radically new forms of divine self-disclosure, then we would be ready to make a shift from being preoccupied with making hermeneutical transfers from the world of the Bible to the world of today, and we would rather find fresh excitement and empowerment in breaking new ground in fresh hermeneutical discovery. What is God saying to the churches today? It cannot be that the ecumenical movement is caught in the trap of using the word of God like a stuck record for nearly two thousand years.

Six. We must take seriously the fact that the mandate of the Risen Christ to the eleven apostles, the pioneers of the Early Church, barricaded by fear in a second-floor room, was to go out into the open and extend the mission of the Kingdom. *"Receive the Holy Spirit. As my father has sent me, even so I send you."* Jesus started a movement and ended up with an institution. We must make the shift in reversing much of that trend. Ecclesiology must give way to Missiology, a Missiology that is inherent in the Pneumatology we use to support our ecumenical initiatives. The same Spirit who gives unity to believers is the same who sends believers out to make disciples.

Seven. This is not to say that we must abandon our Ecclesiology altogether, but rather that we must de-escalate our ecclesiological emphasis, and at the same time, refocus its efficacy in terms of the Reign of God which Jesus established with his life, death and resurrection. What I mean is, that in addition to proclaiming the Church as a living sign of the coming Reign of God, we should also be persistent in a practical ecclesiology which demonstrates what the Reign of God is not.

Eight. Our practical ecclesiology has often tended to focus attention on the Church as an organization, a social institution that subsists in the marketing and dispensation of moral and spiritual goods and services of unique and immeasurable value. The values we share in the church are eternal, we say, and yet they are still regarded as intensely human. Let us make a shift towards a practical ecclesiology that seeks rather to announce God's validation of human realities, and God's acceptance of humanity in the context of brokenness and social dislocation.

Nine. Practical ecclesiology involves ministry, and issues of ministry have been a major sticking-point in the history of the ecumenical movement. The major historical blot, of course, was the spectacle of one church presumptuously declaring the orders of another church invalid, towards the end of the last century. Ministry has been associated with power and authority in the church, and no other issue provides more universal obstacles than the project of recognition or reconciliation of each other's ministries. We should make every effort to shift away from questions of recognition and reconciliation, and simply get on with the business of joint ministries in the world, while leaving ministries in the church to sort themselves out in two or three generations from now. If we place the major emphasis on the Mission of God, then the mutual affirmation of each other's ministries provides empowerment, but the squabbles over mutual recognition constitutes major hindrances to that Mission.

Ten. The question of ministry itself requires some degree of shift in emphasis. Theologically we have tended to focus on a variety of Greek words in the New Testament to provide us with paradigms for ministry. We traditionally speak of ministry as service. The problem has been that those who claim to serve often end up either being served, or turning their efforts into disservice. Alienation of those to be served often follows. We need to shift towards an understanding of ministry as invitation; inviting not only to the banquet of the Reign of God, but stepping aside to enable those who have been invited to become inviters themselves. Ministry as invitation leads to Christ's table, Ministry as service leads to our own tables, where there is often a scarcity of food for the hungry. My colleague John Pobee of Ghana and Geneva puts it this way: "since ministry is exercised by the whole people of God it amounts to an activity of mutual appreciation, mutual strengthening, cooperative search for God, cooperative search for the human face of God in today's world."[13]

In conclusion, as we seek to move forward the work of ecumenical dialogue and reconstruction, let us hold fast to the firm conviction that, at the very least, we who would seek to believe, and live, and witness together, are not enemies of the Cross of

Christ. We who acknowledge the koinonia that already exists among us, are not pipe dreamers holding out for that which will never come. Let us go forward together as Christians in firm assurance of faith that the Mission of God is too exciting and precious for Christians to attempt it on their own. We need each other, and the memories of our particularity will not hold us in bondage indefinitely. The times are still urgent, the days are still evil, and God is still on the way towards us. Let us go forward together towards an excitingly new and fresh divine-human encounter. This is our life; this is the faith that is ahead of us; this is the witness to which we are called in Christ. In the words of FAITH AND ORDER:

> *"This witness and this cooperation do not belong only to the time of full visible unity. On the road to visible unity the way in which divided Christian communities relate to one another, forbear one another in love, bear one another's burdens, share their spiritual and material goods, serve the world together, stick with the pain that arises out of our differences, even enter one another's pain, witnesses to that unity and that communion towards which they strive." (Faith And Order Working Document, April 1992, Para. 93)*

# CHAPTER TEN

# *GOD SAVE THE CHURCH*

What are we doing on Sunday mornings when we gather together for worship in our churches? What do those church-buildings represent during the rest of the week when they are not frequented by the Sunday morning patrons? What brings us apart from the ordinary world in which we live into a controlled and sanitized environment with all the rituals and ceremonies, the singing and praying, the fellowship and preaching? What is the point of it all? What difference does it make? What would our real world be missing if this kind of activity simply faded away into abject obscurity and quiet disuse? Would our world greatly miss the noise of our solemn and sacred assemblies? In a social context of mindless violence, abuse of innocent children, spousal victimization, and social and ecological irresponsibility, how does a liturgical event really fit? We continue to remind ourselves that the worshipping church is the most conspicuous sign we have that the church is still alive. Yet does not that liturgical activity seem to stick out like a sore thumb in a world going mad?

## *THE MEANING OF WORSHIP*

Why do we worship anyway? We worship because we wish to elevate our ordinary human wills to that which is super-ordinary in our structure of belief, at least for a little while. To will to be in the special presence of God is to seek to elevate the will to a level of transcendence, to reach out for a kind of communion with the divine which we believe to be not only possible, but also desirable for our moral and spiritual health. Someone has said that "God" is a metaphor by which we seek to get in touch with our deepest selves. But for the worshipper who functions daily with a complex system of personal volition, to worship is not to transform a metaphor, but to seek for, and be found by, the God who is very real in our lives. The words of the psalmist about the joy of entering into the presence of the Lord speak to this mystical elevation -- *"I was glad when they said to me, let us go into the house of the Lord."* (Psalm 122:1)

We worship because we wish to consecrate some of our time in special address to God as the Creator and Sustainer of our very beings. The consecration of time which takes place in the context of our market-culture is always of great significance. Time is precious. Time is bankable. We make our living by selling our time, our professional time, our talented time, to those who wish to benefit from our services. To consecrate some of that time to God, without sending God a bill afterwards, is an act of dedication, an act of consecration. Our time is us. To offer up of our time is to offer up of ourselves, especially where there are no tangible and bankable returns on such an investment. The consecration of moments in our lives is a sacred duty which we treasure; it is also a glorious opportunity for rediscovering ourselves in the context of a sacred culture, beyond the control of market forces.

We worship because we need to revalidate our sacred symbols. Ordinary life is full of symbols, and we spend most of our time both securing them and protecting them. They give concrete expression to our inner identity; they mark out our social space; they provide us with social and economic worth, which is then convertible into human currency. To worship then is to continue in the corporate exercise of revalidating the symbols which convey deeper meaning and value in our lives; meaning and value which go beyond the index of the market, and which function in a wider sphere than the other ordinary symbols of daily living. The sacred symbols have a longer life, they also have a timeless quality. They have made generations of worshippers into saints, even if the harsh realities of life confirm that they are still merely sinners. The church functions by means of its symbols, in language and liturgy, in prayer and proclamation, in ritual and recitation, in aesthetic structure and ascetic vigor.

We worship because we need to designate some physical space as sacred. There are so many different types of space in our culture, all of which are determined by their value in the market. Our homes are granted specific significance, based on their location, and the neighborhood they create. We distinguish our ghettos from our suburbs, our alleys from our avenues, our malls from our "mom-and-pops." Our spaces are where we gather for common cause and collective concern. Yet we need sacred spaces in our lives, places where we can feel that we are on holy ground. We have it within our rights to designate any place as sacred, but we prefer to reserve specific spots for such meaning in our lives. To worship at a certain spot is not so much to transform the place as to dedicate ourselves for the moment at that place. Holy people declare themselves to be in the presence of the Holy God wherever they assemble. *"Where two or three are gathered together in my name there am I in their midst."* (Matthew 18:20) Thus the sacred space is determined not by its physical and concrete characteristics, but rather by what we do there when we assemble.

We worship because we wish to make open demonstration of our commitment to the faith by which we live. The act of coming together is in itself an act of public witness that we are not only Christians seeking fellowship with each other, but we are also persons of common faith whose bond of belief is sufficient to generate common action and inspire corporate identity. The market culture which we sustain often requires demonstrations of one kind or another. Sometimes the demonstrations are subversive to the dominant culture, at other times they give comfort and support to its pillars. The testing of power in the market-place, and the lobbying for change in the corridors of power, combine to make the forces of our market culture almost unassailable in our social structures. Nevertheless, the public demonstration of our common religious faith is perhaps the major antidote at our disposal for mounting a counter-cultural demonstration in the market sphere. In other words the worship of power is only counteracted by the power of worship in the public sphere.

We worship because we need to reconfirm in our lives the values of humanity which both provide foundational structure for our own social existence, and create new ways of nurturing the generations on the way. This means that worship not only provides for us a sense of belonging, a sense of value and meaning, and a sense of our spiritual heritage; it also makes possible the coming together of generational boundaries in our society, which help to ensure the continuity of that which is sacred in our traditions. It is this search for continuity which is so important in the life of the church; for the faith by which we live is passed on in living form, and no amount of literary treasure can substitute for the actual traditions of worship which join together young and old. The old adage that religion is caught and not taught is of relevance here, and nowhere is this to be understood more powerfully than in the common experience of worship.

It must also be said however, that we do not worship because we are trying to get to heaven when we die. If that were the case, we would certainly be guilty of engaging in a lifelong exercise of sanctified self-interest, trying to pay up our premiums on an insurance policy, which then becomes due and cashable at our final date of expiration. It is possible to say that worship is the primary activity of heaven, so far as it is said that those in heaven do always behold the face of God. They are said to share in the Beatific Vision, and to worship the Lord of Lords night and day. It is also possible to say that worship is indeed a foretaste of the life of heaven, where we "behold the fair beauty of the Lord as we visit the Lord's temple." But none of this comes close to suggesting that worship on earth is a guarantee for entering the pearly gates, or for sharing in that "pie-in-the-sky."

It seems to me that we would be on much safer (and perhaps holier) ground if we sought to revisit the language about "heaven," and to think of such a term as an indication of our sense of the presence of God wherever we are. To speak of heaven is to speak of God in locative terms, in terms of place; and because we have no other mental frames of reference, we are prone to locate God somewhere. To worship God then, is not to continue the process of application for heavenly status, it is rather to activate that status of heaven which is ours already; it is to acknowledge and respond to that divine reality which is always on the way towards us. It is to bring into our historical consciousness the recognition of our earthly existence as having heavenly significance, and to make present in our midst that mystical affirmation that there is actually nowhere where our God is not. To say that worship then is an intense form of remembering who we really are, and who is really with us, is vastly different from asserting that it is an assured way of getting to where we wish to be "in the sweet by-and-by."

Nor must we be led to the suggestion that worship either ensures protection from the forces of evil, or from the rigors of misfortune, or that it provides the basic infrastructure for social mobility or civic benefit. This is not to suggest that persons do not attend places of worship for various reasons, or that such places are not carefully chosen in the light of ulterior motives, beyond the unconditional love of God. Worship, as a cultural activity, is clearly embraced as we try to meet a variety of personal and social needs. We would be less than fair if we were to question such needs, or challenge the validity of worship in such circumstances. We have the right to call on God for every and anything.

We have the right to engage in religious practices to supplement our feelings of need, or insufficiency, or fear, or loneliness, or uncertainty about the future. We have the right to choose our company carefully, our social circles strategically, or our religious groupings ideologically. We have the freedom, in most cases, to determine whose moral voice and spiritual stature we will bring into a fertile encounter with our own. Yet none of these rights, freedoms, or intentions, can constitute the essence of worship as that which we give, rather than that which we hope to get. To invite persons to share worship with us on the basis of some results to be tangibly derived, therefore, seems to me to be wholly antithetical to the meaning of worship as simply an address to the unseen God. Feelings of exhilaration and holiness at the end of one worship experience are no more indicative of its authenticity than feelings of aridity and boredom at the end of another. Yet while we strive eagerly to generate the former, we should not be led into a state of paranoia at the emergence of the latter.

We need to be very careful to ensure that our culture of worship does not degenerate into a program of staged political events. There is always the drive in the body politic to turn any and every event into some form of political statement. We cannot deny that each worship event does consist, in some way, of a participation in a political and social ethos, and that the political structures of the society either enable, or else inhibit, the act of free worship. Nevertheless, we should not allow ourselves to be lured into removing from that most sacred of all social activities the transcendental, mysterious, and mystical qualities of our social selves, which are so powerfully brought together for affirmation and nurture in acts of genuine worship. The politicization of Christian worship is perhaps the saddest indication that human beings are prepared to be alienated from their strongest sense of being constantly remade in the image of God. For the point of seeking communion with God can be met no more fully than in the sincere address to God, which genuine worship affords us.

Does worship make a difference then? Would the world miss the noise of our solemn assemblies? The answer to both questions is yes. Worship makes a difference because the worshipper is turned inside out, at least for the time being, reaching beyond the visible, tangible and concrete, to find new meaning in the God who calls all that is visible into being. Worship becomes a subversive activity, then, for it actively reverses the normal patterns of human interaction with the things that are visible, and it places a radically new meaning on the value of time and things. Worship makes it possible for us to revolt against our tendencies to absolutize that which is relative, and to relativize that which is absolute.

What of the noise of our sacred assemblies? Do they add to the cacophony of the world? Indeed they do. Yet the cacophony of the world is perhaps the strongest form of protest in which human beings engage to undo the myths of harmony by which we are almost always overwhelmed. The worship of God interrupts the efforts of a world which pretends to offer us some harmony out of the realities of human existence. The worship of God sustains the joyful voice of human dependence on the Source of our being, and on the Hope of our fulfillment. The worship of God joins in that perpetual orchestral symphony, as it were, which ascribes to the Creator the praise from a created order that knows no other.

Worship then cannot be spasmodic, or regulated; neither can it be enforced. Worship is that which envelopes the whole of life, and thus requires the constant and free response to the God who is always on the way towards us, and with us, without cessation or compromise. Worship must be a continuous attitude of heart, mind, will, and relationship; and such is the nature of our life in God that the meaning of worship gives firm expression to what we do beyond the limits of our liturgical acts. This means that our life in the church is not to be distinguished from our life in God, and that the witness of the church is not merely defined by the visible acts of worship, but also by the personal and individual acts of genuine Christian commitment in the lives of all its members. Liturgy from life is truly inseparable. Liturgy from work is also inextricable.

## FROM WORSHIP TO WORK

During the course of our discussion in this book, we have looked at the inescapable duty of the church to be true to its mission from God, to break new ground, to struggle on new frontiers, to engage itself in service with the world for the liberation of the world. We have examined the nature of Christian ministry in several dimensions, and we have suggested in various ways that ministry which seeks to be faithful to the Gospel of Jesus Christ must also be a living sign of the breaking-in of the Kingdom of God. We have discussed the importance of development as an authentic concern for the Christian life, and we have urged the creation of partnerships which will resolutely strive to redress the problems and difficulties which are inherent in the experiences of poverty, hunger, injustice and underdevelopment. In all of this the question must be asked: Is the church at worship thereby equipped to be the church at work? Or, on the other hand, does worship constitute a collective escape by the church from becoming the church at work? How does the church move from worship to work, especially as we recognize that the very word "liturgy" is derived from the word which means "work"?

It seems to me that we might best attempt a brief answer to this question by focussing attention on the triple challenges of Unemployment, Materialism and Pragmatism. These are three basic human problems in our social and political ethos, and together they provide a daily context in which we move back and forth from worship to work, or to no work. They represent some of the common enemies we face in the Christian warfare, for they are almost always associated with the causes of moral decay, human decadence, and social dislocation. They are also critical aspects of our culture; for they fundamentally define our values and social activity; they drive our choices and priorities; they inform our attitudes about each other in our communities; and they influence the scales of hope and fear by which we direct our time, talents and relationships. We need to look at each in turn, as they not only challenge the life and meaning of the church of God, but they also provide for us the major task as we seek to move from worship to work. In other words, when the worshipping church goes to work, it also goes to war, against the social and moral evils of its time.

With respect to Unemployment, we should notice first of all that most of the parables of Jesus referred to some element of work, or labor. Some character or other was involved in productive or responsible activity, whether they were laborers in the vineyard, a sower of the seed, a seeker of the lost coin, a simple shepherd, or an unjust steward. Jesus speaks of God as his Father who is always working (John 5:17). Paul urges us to see ourselves as workers together with Christ. He prides himself as one who works with his own hands. The early church at Thessalonica is to honor those who are hard workers. The history of religious asceticism is replete with examples of those who found it impossible to separate their life of prayer from their life of work. Thus they could often proclaim: laborare est orare, to work is to pray. The active and living faith of the church demands that we make no peace with either idleness or joblessness. Why not?

There is no way in which we can escape from the central task to which Jesus committed himself in his earthly mission; namely, that he had come that all may have life in all of its fullness (John 10:10). Fullness of human life requires at the very least that we are able to meet the basic needs of life - food, shelter, clothing, clean water, education, and civic access. To provide these basic needs we need to be involved in remunerative employment, or at least to be assured of the resources to secure them. Such principles of life are so basic that it is normal for us to assert that to work is a right, and not simply a privilege. Yes, a job is a basic human right, and this is the inherent message of the Gospel to which the church is expected to be unswervingly committed.

Unemployment is therefore an evil in our society which gives rise to other evils; and the spectacle of humans being rendered idle and unproductive by callous indifference, structural inefficiency, or political machination, is a challenge for the mission of the church which would seek to worship a working God. The growing rate of joblessness across our societies should never lull us into complacency, or into a sense of unimaginative powerlessness. More of our people are losing their jobs. Indeed, many of our churches have taken to the current practice of what is euphemistically being called "downsizing." Churches have been increasingly faced with options of deficit budgeting, or budget reductions; and the latter option has often placed many of our faithful people on the streets. Thus, far from being in the forefront of the battle against unemployment, the church has frequently found itself on the frontlines of being an "unemployer."

How then does the worshipping church go to war against unemployment both within its ranks, and in the world at large? It can bear witness against the pain, suffering, and despair experienced by those who have lost their jobs, or those who have had no jobs at all. It can reconstitute itself, not so much as an employment agency, but as a community of active concern in which to find work for others is not an optional extra but a divine command. It can make every effort to encourage its members to use their social, economic, and political privileges for the benefits of those who need jobs. It can use its considerable social influence and moral suasion to generate new patterns of social conscience and economic responsiveness among its members in the industrial and corporate sectors of society.

The church can review the stewardship of its own resources in the light of the need to fight for the unemployed among us, and it can withdraw its fiscal and material support from bodies and groups which advance the evils of unemployment rather than hinder them. It can bring to its search for jobs the same enthusiasm and theological compulsion that it gives to evangelistic campaigns and programs of membership growth. The "Each-one-bring-one" message that looks for new members should be accompanied by the "Each-one-find-one" task that looks for jobs for the jobless, whether they are church-members or not. In short, the church can do much more to fight against the scourge of joblessness in our midst. Yet this scourge is further made worse by the force of materialism in our social ethos.

The worshipping church is called to fight against the evils of <u>Materialism</u>. Materialism is defined as "attention to or emphasis on material objects, needs, and considerations, with a disinterest in or rejection of spiritual values."[1] Materialism puts profit before people. It treats matter as being of ultimate significance, and creates in its adherents the thirst for more and more. It lifts the joys of <u>having</u> to greater heights of value than the challenge of <u>being</u>. It reduces the duty of <u>sharing</u> to a form of self-centered activity. It makes no mistake about the conviction that one's life does indeed consist in the abundance of things which one possesses, or can acquire. It feeds on various manifestations of greed and avarice. It preys on the base instincts of human weakness - gambling, theft, dishonesty, envy, and lust - and it brings into the open those underlying feelings of insecurity which rob humanity of its real worth and dignity. The Gospel of Jesus Christ calls on us as a church to witness against all these tendencies in our common culture.

In his recent book, The Catholic Ethic And The Spirit Of Capitalism, the Roman Catholic scholar Michael Novak claims that "'the true moral strength of capitalism lies in its promotion of human creativity,' and that a democratic capitalist society, however imperfect, is 'perhaps the most responsive to the social implications of the Gospels yet developed by the human race.'"[2] To this very amazing suggestion Kenneth Woodward made this insightful comment:

> *"This is theological cheerleading of the baldest type. Mr. Novak has never worked in the milieu he romanticizes. His book says nothing about the disruptions to family life demanded of ambitious executives; of the ruthless dispatch of colleagues by competitors on the way up the corporate ladder; of American workers displaced by companies in search of cheaper, foreign labor; of the get-rich-quick ethics of Wall Street; of the blindness of the marketplace to values that transcend its own."*[3]

There can certainly be no doubt that the spirit of capitalism gives life to the forces of materialism, and vice-versa; and that even if the ethic of capitalism can now be dubbed both Catholic and Protestant (Max Weber notwithstanding), materialism is still a basic form of human bondage.

Can the worshipping church go to work against it, especially where so many of its members are caught in the throes of its effect? Since most people seem to concede that materialism is an unassailable spiritual force, is there any point in trying to fight it? Yes, at the very least, we can try to renounce its hold on us. We can take the sacramental life of our worship beyond the walls of our churches, and try to incarnate the sacramental dimensions of human life in the ordinary patterns of our existence. That is to say, the symbolism we give to the sacramental life of our worship should be extended into the other areas of work and living. The meaning of bread and wine, for example, does not end with the Eucharist, but is to be carried over into the other spheres of our material existence, where the staff of life becomes not an end in itself, but a means to a greater end. One of the Eucharistic prayers in the Episcopal Book of Common Prayer includes the following supplication -

> *"Open our eyes to see your hand at work in the word about us. Deliver us from the presumption of coming to this Table for solace only, and not for strength; for pardon only, and not for renewal. Let the grace of this Holy Communion make us one body, one spirit in Christ, that we may worthily serve the world in his name."* (p.372)

We fight materialism in earnest when we seek to give persistent and faithful allegiance to the belief that humankind does not live by bread alone. Quite often, it is the moral incapacity, or spiritual unwillingness, to roll back the forces of materialism, which are often accompanied by the inordinate rise in unemployment in our midst. The "bottom line" is taken by some to be more important than those who are reduced to live at the bottom. For us as Christians, it is critically important that we do not allow all our senses to be resolved into terms of dollars and cents; otherwise the priceless qualities of life may eventually lose their divine significance. The force of materialism often hinders us from the attainment of such a deeply spiritual and eminently ethical ideal. We still have to find an answer to the question which Jesus posed: *"What shall it profit one to gain the whole world and lose one's soul. What shall one give in exchange for one's soul?"* (Matthew 16:26)

The third evil is that of Pragmatism. It is defined as a "philosophical system or movement stressing practical consequences and values as standards by which concepts are to be analyzed and their validity determined."[4] Pragmatism emerged as a philosophical movement at the end of the last century, mainly through the ideas and urgings of Charles Pierce, William James and John Dewey. Dewey's extension of the movement later came to be known as "instrumentalism." This said that ideas were to be regarded as true if they worked in favor of attaining human goals. Dewey was himself a staunch Darwinist. Marcus Singer has suggested that "Pragmatism has been called a typically American philosophy because of its basic optimism, its emphasis on action, and its belief in a future that can be changed by human ideas and efforts. Many people claim that pragmatism expresses the essential American character."[5]

Many persons might be surprised to hear it suggested that this philosophical approach to life is an evil. After all, they might say, is not this the hallmark of common sense? Is not this what it means to be practical? Do we not have an obligation to be realistic, and to follow the logical consequences of that which is patently obvious? Do we not maintain the highest levels of honesty when we try to do what we have to do? Is this not what life is all about? What is wrong with realism, even if it hurts? On the surface, these sentiments appear to be very cogent. They reflect the common feelings of our culture, and they represent a basic approach to the practical demands of daily living. What is wrong with being practical, they ask. Who would dare contradict the arguments of Common Sense?

Yet Pragmatism, as a pillar of the popular culture, thrives on the principle of the zig-zag; it goes up and down, it meanders through a maze of expediency, it throws out those who are no longer useful to its present purposes, and then seeks to restore them in the light of changed conditions. Pragmatism is centered on the proposition that the ends always justifies the means, and that persons are of little worth after they have no more obvious practical value. It promotes what I choose to call the "thingification" of the human species. Pragmatism reduces the value of human life to merely its functional relevance, and holds no brief for the intangible virtues of the human spirit, which we normally claim to be of infinite worth

Pragmatism drives the engines of individualism and competitiveness; it blesses the demons of political expediency, and permeates the very fabric of home and family life with its cold and calculated logic of "outcomes." It gives comfort to the advocates of social Darwinism. In that way, it makes sure that life subsists in the survival of the fittest, and that the socially strong maintain the advantage of getting stronger, while the weak are only expected to grow weaker. Pragmatism does not place any value on sacrifice, or on the social responsibility to protect the unprotected. It rather believes that love, truth, and equity are soft and impractical ideals in social relationships, and that the fundamental axis of social behavior is simply to go with whatever works. For Pragmatism, all virtue is relative, and vice is often very useful.

Thus the Gospel of Common Sense which gives substance to the world of the Pragmatist is antithetical to the Gospel of Jesus Christ, by which we Christians are called to live. The former Gospel proclaims the primacy of the individual, while the latter proclaims the primacy of the community. When the worshipping church goes to war against such an evil therefore, it does so because it is a living community of active faith which cannot lose sight of its nature as the community of the Spirit. To be led by the life-giving Spirit of God is to be led together into constant warfare and witness against such evils as Unemployment, Materialism, and Pragmatism. The worshipping church at work is at one and the same time the church in witness.

## THE WORK OF CHRISTIAN WITNESS

In order to fight the evils outside the church, we are required to acknowledge that the evils within can weaken our resolve to overcome them all. In our first chapter we pointed to some of the crises facing the church today; but we were unable to engage in any discussion on them. Nevertheless there are four critical areas of current conflict in the life of the church to which we wish to briefly draw some attention before we close. These are the issues of Gender, Sexuality, Race, and AIDS. Each issue is highly emotive at the present time, and is being fed by the voracious appetites of the public media.

The issue of Gender is as old as the human species itself, where the role and duties of each branch of the species have always been a settled and unsettling factor in social arrangements. Not only have the feminine dimensions of life been the more critical in the procreation and nurture of life itself, but the masculine dimensions have instinctively sought to fight against the feminine, through the structures of society which they seek to define and control. Why is this so? I believe that some answer can be found in the fact that the role of the masculine has always been more fluid than that of the feminine. It has been riddled with greater mobility, instability and volatility, and saddled with the need to hunt to feed and be fed, while at the same time never ridding itself of the need for feminine nurture and affirmation in some form or other.

Put another way, however, the men who fight against the rights and power of women tend to do so because they really have no instinctual or rational basis on which to deny them. The gender issue in the church is neither theological, ontological, nor traditional. It is essentially ideological, having the force of a visceral and cultural response of the herd to the threat against the only sense of power that men possess. For even muscular (male) power recedes, but maternal power hardly does. The loss of power always threatens the masculine in a way that the feminine never approximates. That is why the ordination of women is for some men nothing short of the loss of masculine power.

So the Gender issue for the church has less to do with the God who made us male and female in God's own image and likeness, and more to do with the God whom we have remade in our own image and likeness. Unfortunately, the church continues to be a faithful engine of the society's norms and customs, rather than a prophetic community seeking to correct them. Can the Gender issue be resolved?

It will be resolved when we begin to accept the complementarity of human life in all of its fullness. It will be resolved when we recognize that the denial of women's rights of access is an unvarnished denial of natural justice, and also an assault on the inherent integrity of that which gave us birth. It will be resolved when we make bold to recognize and affirm our participation in the feminine life of God, emancipating and sustaining our mysterious humanity, and empowering us to affirm the full humanity of the other. It will be resolved when we begin to develop a stronger sense of belonging to Mother Earth and Mother Church, rather than of being their owners. It will be resolved when we earnestly strive to give pride of place to the power of Grace (of God) over the grace of Power (of men).

To delay the inevitable advance of women in reaching the commanding heights of leadership in the church, as they have already done in the community at large, is to shore up for coming generations of males more traumatic experiences of accepting whomever God calls to serve in whatever capacity God wills. The gates of Hell shall not prevail indefinitely.

The issue of <u>Sexuality</u> also constitutes a major preoccupation of the Western churches today. It is directly related to the rising tide of the sexuality agenda among the vocal non-conservatives in our post-modern cultures. There are some who contend that such an agenda is a "symbol of a theological decadence that has sold out to a hostile secular culture."[6] Richard Kew and Roger White predict that "sexuality issues will continue to inflame the tension between liberal and conservative wings of the Church."[7] What has emerged over time to make Sexuality an issue of crisis proportions? Many churches have been exerting feverish efforts to deal with the issue openly. Several studies have been commissioned; several reports have been presented.

The Presbyterian Report, <u>Keeping Body And Soul Together</u>, makes for very interesting reading. In it the authors suggest that -

*"The crisis of sexuality we are experiencing is, in fact, a massive cultural*

*earthquake, a loosening of the hold of an unjust, patriarchal structure built on dehumanizing assumptions, roles, and relationships. This unjust structure stifles human well-being and stands in contradiction to the gospel mandate to love God and neighbor as self."*[8]

It is difficult to identify what the authors regard as the elements of a "massive cultural earthquake" besides their description of the changes, crises, and conflicts of our times converging on our social consciences. However, the Report offered a very significant admission by the authors -

*"As a people of faith who have searched our hearts and minds together, we have learned much in this three-year process. We have been stunned by the scope of sexual pain in our society, saddened by the stories of grief and disillusionment, and repentant that as a denomination we have spoken so cautiously and acted so timidly about sexuality and its many life-centered issues. We have felt sorrow with those who have felt the rejection of this church in their sexual being, and we have felt joy with those who have been extended grace and love by members of this church. We understand with new clarity that human sexuality has an inherent possibility for graciousness and kindheartedness, as well as for alienation and distrust."*[9]

The explosion of the debate within the church will undoubtedly continue to have an incisive impact on the way members of the church relate to each other. Members will be marked out by their orientation, their family connections, their social labels, their ideological positions, and their personal posture or deportment. The issue will continue to generate incalculable heat and uncontrolled emotions. Those in the church who would seize the Gallio option (in caring for none of these things), will do the church a great disservice if they attempt to insulate themselves, or else seek to escape from the pain and the possibility of this important issue. Why?

Because the issue has emerged as a major source of disclosure of that which for centuries has been smothered or concealed by the sophisticated arrogance of the rich and the powerful, or else deviously disguised under the cover of cultural superiority. That is to say, there was a time in Western cultural history when it was only the sexuality of the slaves, or their descendants, which was the issue of the day. The stereotype of the black male and his sexual prowess was the symbol of the worst form of violence from which the white planters sought to protect their families. Yet the enslaved and their descendants were never protected from the ravaging sexuality of the planters themselves. The planters' sexuality in Western history was a far more dangerous weapon against African humanity than the whip on the backs of our forefathers and foremothers. The irony in the current debate is that it is being waged more actively by the descendants of the enslavers than by those of the enslaved. The historical dimensions and implications of the sexuality debate must not be ignored in the church.

The issue seeks to tell the story of how humanity has been attempting to deal "uncomfortably" with the truth about itself and its endowments. Sexuality embraces that which is most deeply human; it envelops everyone, regardless of race or gender; it is inextricably bound up with the procreation and gift of life; it defies the accidents of birth in persons, and affirms the inherent qualities of what it means to be truly human; it calls on all persons to discover who they really are; it gives centrality of place to that most mysterious element in all creation, the human body itself. Sexuality is no respecter of persons, and it offers no compromises to anyone's wishes. It links together the forces of love, and it makes possible a feeling of spiritual warmth and passionate relationship with a God whom we can never see, hear, or feel. We love God with all of our being - sexuality included.

The church must seek relentlessly to rescue the human family from the onslaught of sexual violence and abuse, from wanton cultural promiscuity, and from the commercialization of sex in our modern culture. The general unwillingness in the society to separate the mystification of Sex, from that of Money and Power, constitutes a major assault on the sanctity of the human spirit. The Sexuality issue is important because the church must help us to teach our children the moral skills of determining right from wrong in matters of such vital importance, and to set before them the values and principles by which they will hopefully clean up the mess which our generation has selfishly accumulated. The trends of our times clearly indicate that if the church reneges on the Sexuality issue, no other body in our culture is equipped to deal with it adequately, and the quality of human family life might be irreparably damaged.

The issue of Race is as old as the intervention of the Europeans into the Americas at the end of the fifteenth century. Western civilization was designed on the premise that persons of darker hue were to be perpetually subservient to persons of European descent. Enough has already been written about the significance of Columbus for the New World in the history of Racism, that no further discussion is required on that score. The one assertion which never seems to win any detractors in our social discourse is that racism is alive and well. Andrew Hacker says that "the significance of racism lies in the way it consigns certain human beings to the margins of society, if not painful lives and early deaths. In the United States, racism takes its highest toll on blacks. No white person can claim to have suffered in such ways because of ideas that may be held about them by some black citizens."[10]

The issue of Race continues to thrive in the church. It has often brought many congregations into being because one ethnic grouping found it desirable to break away into a separate congregation along racial lines. It has stood in the way of qualified candidates being considered for ecclesiastical positions on account of their color. It has given rise to gross insensitivity of language, attitudes and actions within congregations, and it has brought many promising relationships to painful and explosive ends. Racism is an evil, and no amount of racism audits, or official policy pronouncements, or carefully selected commissions or task forces, will ever bring about that radical conversion of heart, mind, will, and social structure, which alone can rid our society from this cancerous scourge.

Although we take no comfort in the following words of Derrick Bell, we consider that they constitute something of a real challenge for the church. Bell says: "racism lies at the center, not the periphery; in the permanent, not in the fleeting; in the real lives of black and white people, not in the sentimental caverns of the mind."[11] He goes on to suggest that the appropriate response to this reality lies in engagement and commitment, which "connote service." Bell continues -

> *"We must first recognize and acknowledge (at least to ourselves) that our actions are not likely to lead to transcendent change and may indeed, despite our best efforts, be more help to the system we despise than to the victims of that system which we are trying to help. Then, and only then, can that realization and the dedication based on it lead to policy positions and campaigns that are less likely to worsen conditions for those we are trying to help and more likely to remind the powers that be that out there are persons like us who are not only not on their side but determined to stand in their way."*[12]

It would be a travesty of the Christian faith, as well as the Gospel of Jesus Christ, if the church were to resign itself to the permanence of racism among its members.

The final issue is that of <u>AIDS</u>. We have been accustomed to placing more emphasis on the preaching and teaching ministry of Jesus, while neglecting the implications of the healing ministry. The significance of the healing miracles in the Gospel is that Jesus was able to demonstrate the power of God where ordinary people believed themselves to be in the inescapable bondage of demons and disease. AIDS holds us in that form of bondage at present. John Snow has suggested that: "What AIDS is teaching us spiritually is ... a culture healthy for human beings mitigates the fear of death, constantly, by its customs and rituals ... AIDS has brought our mortality out of hiding, and made it very difficult to deny."[13]

Not only does it bring out our fear of death, it also brings out lack of faith and loving concern for those who are living with the disease, or for those who are related to them. The way in which the church has attempted to draw circles around its ministry to the AIDS crisis has left much to be desired, and the unwillingness to educate its members about the realities of the scourge makes fear a more prominent force in the church than faith.

It seems to me that there are five critical factors to which the church must seriously address its attention. One, the church must develop programs for educating its membership, as well as the community it serves, about the causes, symptoms, control, and prevention of the disease. Two, as the Body of Christ, the church has to become the compassionate community to which it is summoned by the healing presence of the Risen Jesus. For if those who are visited by the disease cannot find compassion and a caring response within the church, where else must they turn? Three, the church must devote some of its resources to help churches in other parts of the world where the disease is raging rampant; especially in several parts of Africa. Four, we must take seriously the challenge of the World Council Of Churches to become in every respect the Healing Community. The Central Committee's Hearing On AIDS produced its Report in 1987 in which the following challenge was issued:

> 'The Aids (si^) crisis challenges us profoundly to be the Church in deed and in truth: <u>to be the church as a healing community</u>. Aids is heartbreaking and challenges the churches to break their own hearts, to repent of inactivity and of rigid moralisms. Since Aids cuts across race, class, gender, age, sexual orientation and sexual expression, it challenges our fears and exclusions.' The healing community itself will need to be healed by the forgiveness of Christ.[14]

Five, now that significant advances are being made in medical research about the HIV virus and the AIDS disease, the church must be actively involved in promoting both the research and the benefits of the newly discovered knowledge.

Let us not forget those beautiful words of Mother Theresa uttered in New York in 1986 about persons living with AIDS. She said: "Each one of them is Jesus in a distressing disguise."[15] She gives us strong echoes of Jesus who has reminded us that wherever we minister to the least of his brothers and sisters in their destitute state, we are actually ministering to him. May God save the church as it strives unconditionally to save God's creatures.

## BEGINNING TOMORROW TODAY

We began this book with a question about the church. We asked in our first chapter "Can The Church Be Saved?" We were concerned to discuss the priorities to which the church would need to address itself if it were to continue to be an agency of divine salvation in the world. The church constantly needs to be a changed agent if it is to be an agent of God's salvific change. We went on to examine the nature of the God who had called the church into being, first through the ancient people of Israel and then through the followers of Christ. The God who calls into being also calls into covenant, and that covenantal relationship is most powerfully experienced through the creative encounter of God in the changes of our history.

We looked at the church in terms of its mission, and we took note of the fact that the doctrine of God and the doctrine of mission were inextricably related, for the Covenant God was also the sending God. We were to understand that the purpose of mission was always to discover the purpose of mission. The church was expected to be on the move through its historical encounter with world history; for there was no difference between world history and God's salvation history. Such a mission meant that there would always be new frontiers to discover, new horizons to be created, new possibilities to be risked for the sake of the Gospel and the ministry of Jesus Christ.

The church's concern for the poor and oppressed is not to be considered as an optional extra, but rather as that which is crucial to a faithful fulfillment of the mandate of Jesus in the Gospel. To be actively involved in working for the development of peoples, particularly in the poorer regions of the world, is a dimension of Christian witness and service to which the church must constantly challenge its members. Such participation in development calls for the creation of networks and partnerships in the struggle against poverty in the world. Care must be taken that our efforts do not eventuate in working against the poor. The church must constantly become a catalyst for the creation of coalitions of compassion, as it struggles to bear witness to the transforming love of the crucified Christ.

To love the Lord our God with heart, mind, soul, and strength, and our neighbor as ourselves, is almost the whole duty of the Christian church. The rest of the duty of the church is to worship that God who calls us into being, and who is always meeting us in liberating truth and empowering hope. To worship that God is to be filled with the vision of the world which belongs only to God, the principalities and powers of the age notwithstanding. The primary duty of the worshipping church then is to glorify that God whose presence daily makes new the way that leads to salvation.

Thus the church is not only a community on the way to salvation, but a community which offers God's salvation to the world. It is the vision of the saving God at work in the world which alone can offer hope to an otherwise meaningless form of contemporary existence. Even within the church that sense of meaninglessness can often overwhelm those whose faith is under siege by the violent and terrifying pressures of the age. The words of Cardinal Joseph Bernardin offer us some helpful insight: "The life of faith needs to be presented as an enhancement of all that we know, not in isolation from the frontiers of human knowledge and creativity."[16]

When we seek to isolate ourselves from the totality of God's loving created order, and withdraw from the frontiers of knowledge and creativity, it is then that we are overtaken by this sense of meaninglessness, and are quick to cry out in despair: "God! Save the Church!" But, when we take the risk of being fully involved with God's One, Holy, Catholic, and Apostolic mission, breaking new ground for the Gospel, and working with God in making all things new, through our radical repentance and constant obedience, the glories of God's brightness are most powerfully evident in the church's worship, work, and witness. It is then that the celestial angels rejoice with their unending song of praise: GOD SAVE THE CHURCH! May God's angels never cease to make their joyful song.

# Postscript

THE QUESTION THAT INSPIRED the title of this book in 1994, some quarter of a century ago, is still very much alive and pertinent in this era of sweeping changes and grave uncertainties. *Can God Save the Church?* The discussions that were raging throughout the religious communities then were primarily concerned with the priorities for mission and evangelism. They were focusing on the meaning of justice and human equality, the just demands of the marginalized and the oppressed, and the rights and freedoms of gays, lesbians, and transgendered persons. HIV-AIDS was still rampant, grave health disparities prevailed, and the criminal justice system still worked mainly in favor of the rich, white, and powerful. Gun violence continued to be on the increase, while the gaps between the very rich and the very poor were widening exponentially.

The year 2020 has been for the entire globe a most horrible and traumatic experience; and 2021 has dawned with little hope of being any better. At the core of it all has been the devastating surge of the coronavirus officially named COVID-19 by the World Health Organization (WHO). The global statistics of human suffering and loss have been truly unimaginable, and the negative effects that have been wreaked on systems, cultures, institutions, relationships, opportunities, and expectations are unfathomable. The ancient fears of plagues, pestilence, and famine have now been overtaken by the new word "pandemic". Humanity has become mortally aware of the commonality of its predicament that the virus is no respecter of persons. High and low, rich and poor, colored and non-colored, citizens and aliens, we have all become fearfully aware of our fragile vulnerability.

Many have been moved to reflect openly on the significance of these experiences, not only for their historical ripple effects on the social, economic, and medical disruptions on human well-being, but also on the religious, moral, and spiritual reorientations that will have emerged over time. There have been many creative ways explored and expressed in a vast array of human endeavors, not least of which have been the adjustments in religious gatherings and ways of worship. The experiments in new forms of liturgy have given rise to some novel ways of theological justification, such as the expanded claims of sacramentalism expressed through virtual technology, as well as what it means to be a member of the church that one has never physically attended. Church attendance has both changed and expanded right across the globe which both excites and challenges the traditional church, as church leaders grapple with connecting with the future flock of the faithful.

Zoom, YouTube, Facebook, and other streaming devices have become agents and channels of sacramental and spiritual efficacy. Countries the world over have been forced to mandate "lockdowns", but religious communities have responded by insisting that this could not possibly mean being "locked out". Funerals, Weddings, Eucharists, Committee meetings, Concerts, Visitations, Rehearsals, Consultations, and other forms of religiously oriented activities and programs have all been subject to the rigors of Pandemic prevention. Some have referred to all of this as a "New Normal", while others have rather insisted that it is a "New Reality". For all of us, however, it is perhaps an incontrovertible prediction that life will never be the same again.

The latter half of the past decade has witnessed a virtual sea change in the affairs of societies and cultures, in attitudes of religious leaders and denominational groupings, as well as in some long-held traditions and customs. Apart from the rapid rise in global warming and the accompanying concerns and controversies about climate change, new forms of dependency and indebtedness have created dislocations of national expectations and fresh surges of human social deficits. It is in the areas of moral, ethical, and social decline, however, that the concerns of this book still must be addressed.

No one could ever have imagined that we would ever witness the spectacle of a white police officer forcing his knee on the neck of a Black man, George Floyd, unarmed and shackled, and lying on the ground. As Floyd called out for his mother, he cried out "I can't breathe!" But that was not enough to stop that modern-day form of lynching. Were it not for the that young African American woman Darnella Frazier, who used her cellphone camera to video record that horrible scene of police brutality in Minneapolis, the whole world may not have been able to respond with such a global protest to the historic disaster.

No one could ever have imagined that a woman, an African American, resting in her own home, perhaps after a hard day at work, would have been attacked by a contingent of police officers who had invaded the wrong house. She was shot to death in a raid that had obviously gone wrong. Her name was Breonna Taylor. The memory of this tragic event has created its own defining moment in the recent American historic narrative when it is linked to the memory of the George Floyd brutal disaster, mentioned in the previous paragraph. The bodies of Black men and Black women have continued to bear the brunt of White supremacy and comfort, and the brutality of White power. The question that rages in the minds of millions is this: can Black and Brown bodies find any space or place of haven anywhere in these United States? Even though the theme of "Black Lives Matter" has taken on a global life and affirmation all of its own, the critical question centers around "mattering to whom"? In the meantime, there are those who would continue to make the claim that the persistence of White supremacy has been rooted and shaped by the underlying prevalence of Christian supremacy.

The spectacle of the White police officer holding the back of the vest of a Black man, Jacob Blake, as he tried to enter his car where his children were seated in the back, and firing no fewer than five gunshots into his back gives unmistakable demonstration of White utter disdain for Black bodies. The tragic end of Elijah Jovan McClain a twenty-three-year-old Black therapist in Aurora, Colorado who was placed in a chokehold by the police on my birthday, August 24$^{th}$, 2019, as he quietly returned home from a nearby shop, further readily comes to mind. So too does the shooting of Ahmaud Arbery on February 23$^{rd}$, 2020, who was allegedly chased by White men in a South Georgia neighborhood. Not only did it highlight the horrors of racial profiling in America, it also brought into national focus again the interpretation given to the laws of so-called "self-defense" (Stand Your Ground), as well as the unmitigated arrogance of White supremacy that gives license to the pervasive practice of citizen policing. The explosive emergence of the "Karen" phenomenon of White women calling the police to arrest Black bodies all over the country has more than exacerbated the societal maladies of the present age. The vestiges of slavery, lynching, and Jim Crow have manifested themselves in so many contemporary forms and fashions that the ubiquitous and pernicious surges of systemic racism and social inequality have literally come to define the harsh realities of our times.

No one could ever have imagined that the United States Capitol Building in Washington, DC, which has been heralded historically as the majestic bastion of American democracy, and the citadel of the world's greatest deliberative body (the United States Congress), would have become the theater for the most violent assault on democracy itself. On the Feast of the Epiphany, January 6$^{th}$, 2021, violent mobs left a rally that was staged in front of the White House, where the then-President of the United States was the principal speaker, and invaded the hallowed walls of the Capitol. They ransacked the houses of both the House of Representatives and the Senate in a violent attempt to undo the results of a national election that had been held some two months earlier. Some have referred to that horrible event as "domestic terrorism". Many others have called it an "insurrection", while others have gone as far as calling it an "attempted coup." Labels of that historic tragedy are not as important as the legacy that has erupted into the national consciousness (epiphany) and the annals of the American mythos (human story). While some cynics have opined that America's chickens have "come home to roost," others have declared that the presumed inviolability of America's innocence has been irrevocably exposed. The idea of the American democratic societal experiment is going terribly in the wrong direction as a fragile nation grapples with the future of a "more perfect union." One wonders if these are the results of the Trumpian *Make America Great Again* political machinery and ideology that is often masked as a determination to make America "White" again.

In writing about the Myth of American Exceptionalism, the Reverend Peter Marty of *The Christian Century* has offered the following insight: "To believe that moral values and virtuous leadership are self-enforcing is to fool ourselves. To suppose that malignant narcissism is harmless, that authoritarian behavior is tolerable, or that cruel nationalism is somehow congruent with our founding principles only contributes to national shame and global humiliation."[1] This observation is cogently indicative of the climate, atmosphere, and cultures that have converged to render the realities of our times both culturally explosive and morally challenging. The riots that erupted on January 6th in the American historical narrative have brought into full focus the contradictions between religious nationalism and structural racism.

Nowhere has this been in evidence more than the stark comparison between the tepid police response to the riots on Capitol Hill in January 2021, where at least five people have lost their lives, and the harsh responses to the "Black Lives Matter" peaceful demonstrations near the White House in July 2020. For, whereas the 2021 riots were plentifully placarded with slogans of religious self-righteousness, extolling the power of guns, guts, God, and Jesus, the 2020 demonstrations were laced with signs and placards appealing for justice, equality, peace, and the end to racism. This means that, with both crowds claiming the moral ascendancy of religious symbolism and Christian social principles, the title of this book still holds: *Can God Still Save the Church?*

Two recent statements from leaders in the Anglican Communion ring true in the contemporary climate. One deals with the rise of Christian nationalism in America, while the other reflects very cogently on the persistence of racism in South Africa, but undoubtedly has global relevance. The Right Reverend Michael Curry, who happens to be the first Black Presiding Bishop of the Episcopal Church in America (and who we hope will not be the last), has been very strident about the dangers for Christianity inherent in the culture and expansion of Christian nationalists. They had been very prominent in the crowds of the infamous Insurrection on January 6th, 2021, where

---

1. Peter W. Marty, "Crumbling Myth of American Exceptionalism," *Christian Century*, January 25, 2021, https://www.christiancentury.org/article/editorpublisher/crumbling-myth-american-exceptionalism, para. 5.

the name of Jesus was widely displayed on banners ("Jesus 2020"). Bishop Curry has urged that: "We must counter the negative perversions of Christianity and of our humanity with an affirmative, positive way of being Christian. Christianity must re-center itself on the teachings, the example, and the spirit of Jesus of Nazareth. The Bishop went on to say that: Christianity has been held hostage. We must reclaim it. We have to counter the negative with the positive, because the positive is there. We also have to embody it."[2]

The other statement came from Archbishop Thabo Makgoba of the Anglican Church in South Africa. He affirmed that:

> The church can't be partisan; I can't go and stand for political office and say I'll advance the biblical texts in politics. Some can do that. But I think our true vocation is to say the rule of God is at hand, and what is God's kingdom ... in contextual issues? We can do that in advocacy, and then we can give agency to particular groups that are affected by that racism and exclusion. We can name the evil that is racism, because we know that racism reduces the God in you and the God in me into some smaller God, and makes one race's God bigger than who God created us to be.[3]

As this third decade of the twenty-first century gets on its way, therefore, we are confronted with a multiplicity of pandemics while the realities of injustice, inequality, insensitivity, inertia, incompetence, and insurrection continue to confront the mission of the Church. The pandemic of disease is added to the other pandemics of discrimination, deprivation, depression, divisiveness, and domestic violence. Hovering over all these realities and pandemics is the increasing surge of death from the ravages of COVID-19 and suicides. And yet, the Church continues to proclaim a Gospel of the One (Jesus Christ), whose stated mission was that he had come among us to bring life in all of its fullness (John 10:10).

This updated version of the book originally conceived in 1994 takes a fresh view through new lenses of old and current twenty-first century issues that cause us to tremble in trepid and tumultuous waters, and to once again seek the solace of a savior. As we slowly creep forward during a time of resolute hope with infinite confidence, may the Gospel of God's forgiveness be forcefully proclaimed and consistently practiced. May the Gospel of God's freedom be passionately expressed and courageously

---

2. Kirk Petersen, "PB, Others Speak Out Against Christian Nationalism," https://livingchurch.org/2021/01/28/pb-and-others-speak-out-against-christian-nationalism/, para. 9.

3. Matt Gardner, "'We Can Name the Evil That Is Racism': A Conversation with Archbishop Thabo Makgoba," *Anglican Journal*, February 1, 2021, https://www.anglicanjournal.com/we-can-name-the-evil-that-is-racism-a-conversation-with-archbishop-thabo-makgoba/, para. 30.

advanced. May the Gospel of God's future, in the face of the countervailing storms of the present times, be faithfully extolled and unapologetically embraced. So may the Church, as the people of God, the household of faith, and the community of God's enlivening Spirit continue relentlessly along the challenging paths of worship, work, and witness, giving daily embodiment to the full meaning of its family prayer: *Thy Kingdom come, Thy will be done, On Earth, as it is done in Heaven.*

Kortright Davis, Kensington, Maryland, USA
February, 2021

# ENDNOTES

## Chapter One

1. J. Herbert Kane, "My Pilgrimage In Mission," *International Bulletin of Missionary Research* (Vol. 11, No. 3 July 1987), p.132
2. David Bosch, "Vision For Mission", *International Review of Mission*, (Vol. LXXVI No. 301, Jan. 1987), p.14
3. Walbert Buhlmann, With Eyes To See, (Orbis Books, New York, 1990), p.146
4. Buhlmann, op. cit., p.147
5. See *The International Review of Mission*, (Vol. LXXXVI No. 303, July 1987) p.400
6. J. N. J. Kritzinger, "Black Eschatology And Christian Mission", *Missionalia*, (Vol. 15, No. 1, April 1987) p.23
7. Buhlmann, op. cit., p.157
8. See Walbert Buhlmann, op. cit., p.14

## Chapter Two

1. George E. Mendenhall & Gary A. Herion, "Covenant", Anchor Bible Dictionary, Vol.I, p.1201
2. Heinz Kruse, "David's Covenant". Vetus Testamentum) (Vol. XXXV, N0. 2, April, 1985), p.158
3. G.E. Mendenhall, "Covenant", The Interpreter's Dictionary Of The Bible, Vol. I (Abingdon, Nashville, 1981), p.719
4. Klaus Baltzer, The Covenant Formulary, (Fortress Press, Philadelphia, 1971), p.112
5. Delbert R. Hillers, Covenant: The History Of A Biblical Idea, (Johns Hopkins Press, Baltimore, 1969), p.178
6. David Hartman, A Living Covenant, (The Free Press, New York, 1985), p.3
7. Bruce V. Malchow, "The Messenger Of The Covenant In Malachi 3:1" Journal Of Biblical Literature (Vol. 103, No. 2, June, 1984), pp. 252-53
8. G.E. Mendenhall, "Covenant", p.722
9. G.E. Mendenhall, "Covenant", p.723
10. Mendenhall & Herion, op. cit. p.1198
11. Klaus Baltzer, op. cit., p.180
12. Delbert R. Hillers, op.cit., p.4
13. Mendenhall & Herion, op. cit., p.1201
14. Ibid.
15. David Hartman, op.cit., p.4
16. Charles S. McCoy, When Gods Change: Hope For Theology, (Abingdon, Nashville, 1980), p.179

17. Charles S. McCoy, op. cit., p.189
18. J. Philip Wogaman, *Faith And Fragmentation: Christianity For A New Age*, (Fortress Press, Philadelphia, 1985), p.56
19. I am using the term 'bargain' in this discussion, not to denote something cheap and inconsequential, but rather in terms of an agreed understanding between parties that is characterized by a spirit of give and take.
20. David Hartman, op.cit., pp.262-63
21. Mendenhall & Herion, op. cit., p.1201

## Chapter Three

1. See International Review of Mission, (Vol. LXXIII, No 289, January, 1984), p.67.
2. See Gerald H. Anderson and Thomas F. Stransky, eds., *Mission Trends No. 1*, (New Jersey: Paulist Press, 1974), p.56
3. *Your Kingdom Come: Mission Perspectives* - Report of the World Conference on Mission and Evangelism, Melbourne, Australia, 12-25 May, 1980 (Geneva: CWME, World Council of Churches, 1980), p.176
4. Cited in J. G. Davies, *Worship and Mission* (New York: Association Press), 1983, p.98
5. Wolfhart Pannenberg, *The Church*, (Philadelphia: The Westminster Press, 1983), p.10
6. Ibid., p.11
7. Ibid., p.13.
8. See International Review of Mission, (Vol. LXXII, No. 288, October, 1983), p.577
9. Jurgen Moltmann, *The Church In The Power Of The Spirit*, (London: SCM Press, 1977), p.352
10. Ibid., p.361
11. Pannenburg, *Church*, p.53
12. Davies, *Worship*, p.36.
13. David J. Bosch, *Witness To The World*, (Atlanta: John Knox Press, 1980), p.18.
14. See Alan Richardson and John Bowden eds., *The Westminster Dictionary of Christian Theology*, (Philadelphia: The Westminster Press, 1983), p.374.
15. See International Review of Mission, (Vol.LXXIII, No. 289, January, 1984), p.32.
16. James F. White, *Sacraments As God's Self-Giving*, (Nashville: Abingdon, 1983), p.109.
17. White, *Sacraments*, p.110
18. Ibid.
19. Wolfhart Pannenberg, *Christian Spirituality*, (Philadelphia: The Westminster Press, 1983) p.70.

20. Carl E. Braaten, *The Flaming Center*, (Philadelphia: Fortress Press, 1977), Ch.1.
21. Ibid., p.34.
22. Bosch, Witness, p.507.

## Chapter Four

1. Quoted by Joyce M. Lumsden, "Robert Love And Jamaican Politics", (Unpublished Ph.D. Dissertation, UWI, Kingston, Jamaica, 1987), p.50. I am immensely indebted to Dr. Lumsden for most of my information about Dr. Love, and I eagerly look forward to her Dissertation being published.
2. See Lumsden, op. cit., p.66
3. See Lumsden, op. cit., p.349
4. See Lumsden, op. cit., p.342
5. See Lumsden, op. cit., p.345
6. See Lumsden, op. cit., p.243
7. See Lumsden, op. cit., p.304
8. See Lumsden, op. cit., p.284
9. See Lumsden, op. cit., p.210
10. See, Lumsden, op. cit., p.334
11. See Lumsden, op. cit., p.293
12. See Lumsden, op. cit., p.296
13. See Lumsden, op. cit., p.347
14. A.C. Terry-Thompson, *The History Of The African Orthodox Church*, (Beacon Press, New York, 1956), p.50
15. See William Montgomery Brown, *The Crucial Race Question*, 2nd edition, (Arkansas Churchman's Publishing Co., Little Rock, 1907), p.273
16. See Brown, op. cit., p.277
17. Ibid.
18. See Brown, op. cit., p.279
19. See Brown, op. cit., p.280
20. See Brown, op. cit., p.281
21. See Brown, op. cit., p.282
22. W.M. Brown, *The Catholic Church And The Color Line*, (1910), p.17
23. *Annual Report Of The Board Of Missions Of The Protestant Episcopal Church In The U. S. A.*, (1912), p.40
24. Randall K. Burkett, *Black Redemption*, (Temple University, Philadelphia, 1978), p.166
25. Burkett, op. cit., p.168
26. Burkett, op. cit., p.173
27. Burkett, op. cit., p.175
28. Burkett, op. cit., p.176
29. Burkett, op. cit., p.177

30. Burkett, op. cit., p.180
31. "Bishop R.G. Barrow: His Life In The A.M.E. Church" Transcript of Interview with Fred & Sylvia Talbot, (Barbados, n.d.), mimeo, p.7
32. "Bishop R.G. Barrow.." p.9
33. "Barrow" p.12
34. "Barrow" p.13
35. "Barrow" p14
36. "Barrow" p21
37. Sixteenth Episcopal District Of The African Methodist Episcopal Church, Compiled by R.R. Wright Jr., (1964), p.103
38. The Negro Churchman, (New York, Vol.V, No.9, October, 1927), p.1

## Chapter Seven

1. "Washington Post", February 16, 1986, p.C1
2. David C. Korten, Getting To The 21st Century, (Kumarian Press, West Hartford, 1990), p.4
3. World Bank, World Development Report 1991, (Oxford University Press, New York, 1991), p.1
4. Robert Bellah et. al., ed. Habits of the Heart, (University of California Press, Berkeley, 1985), p. 295

www.ingramcontent.com/pod-product-compliance
Lightning Source LLC
Chambersburg PA
CBHW081132170426
43197CB00017B/2834